Read what others are saying about this book

"Dan has done an 'amazing' amount of research along with sharing his 'extensive global travel experiences.' If you want to be a savvy and happier air traveler, this is a must-read."
--**Howard Putnam, former CEO, Southwest Airlines and author of** *The Winds of Turbulence.*

"I've flown more than 3 million miles and was amazed by how many new ideas Dan's book gave me to: save time, save money, and save hassles. Don't take off without the *Air Travel Handbook.*"
--**W Mitchell, past president of the Global Speakers Federation and author of** *It's Not What Happens to You, It's What You Do About It.*

"Peace of mind may be the greatest benefit if you travel, especially overseas. An aware traveler is a protected traveler."
--**Norman Zalfa, past Director of Security, ITT Europe.**

"This is the best book on travel I've ever seen—and I wrote one myself."
--**Tim Gard, million mile flyer, professional speaker on air travel and author of** *Just Plane Funny.*

"Dan Poynter flies so much he's practically in orbit and these are the resources that make his life easier. Passengers! Want to make your life easier? Get this eBook."

—Diana Fairechild, former international chief flight attendant who flew 10 million miles.

"Dan Poynter has finally collected, in one volume for passengers, information they need to identify and avoid known hazards, and implement their personal risk avoidance options. This book is an education both for experienced travelers, and for those who have not become familiar with the seamier side of international travel."
--Ira Rimson, retired forensic engineering specialist in aircraft accident reconstruction and analysis.

"I LOVE this book. Not only does Dan give great and pertinent advice, he includes the links. As that info as is updated, so is the book. Brilliant! This goes with me on every trip now."
--Beth Terry, CSP, Author & Speaker.
Address: 38,000 feet over Phoenix.

"This book looks great, Dan takes his own advice very well -- "write what you know"!
--Arlene Prunkle, PenUltimate Editorial Services, Vancouver, Canada.

"Dan is the most experienced world traveler I know. Anyone who travels, a little or a lot, needs Dan's *Air Travel Handbook*. It's packed with 215 pages of great tips and tricks that will make your air travels much easier, and even lots of fun. Anyone who travels can benefit from Dan's wealth of experience and knowledge."
--John Cali, author, publisher, traveler.

"Dan's new book, the *Air Travel Handbook*, is a gem for travelers and travel writers. The hundreds of inside factoids and processes should make your trip logistics quicker and easier. There's a ton of linked info too that will stay current and usable whenever you go. A great, deductible source you can carry digitally anywhere."
--Gordon Burgett, author of the *Travel Writer's Guide*

"An extremely valuable resource for air travelers. It is worthy of every penny you spend on it. Dan is very detail-oriented, and this shows in his books. If he decides to write on a subject, you can count on him to do VERY comprehensive research work, and covers EVERYTHING you need to know about it."
--Gang Chen, AIA, LEED AP BD+C, author of books on various LEED exams, architecture, and landscape architecture

"When once you have tasted flight,
you will forever walk the earth with
your eyes turned skyward,
for there you have been,
and there you will always long to
return."

--Leonardo da Vinci, (1452 - 1519)
Italian engineer, painter, and sculptor.

Dan Poynter's

Air Travel Handbook

Tips, Tricks, & Secrets on Flying

Para Publishing,
Santa Barbara, CA, USA.

Air Travel Handbook

Tips, Tricks, & Secrets on Flying
by Dan Poynter

Para Publishing
PO Box 8206, Santa Barbara, CA 93118-8206 USA
http://ParaPublishng.com, http://AirTravelHandbook.com

All rights reserved. No part of this book may be reproduced or transmitted in any form or by any means, electronic or mechanical, including photocopying, recording or by any information storage and retrieval system, without written permission from the author, except for the inclusion of brief quotations in a review.

Copyright © 2011 by Dan Poynter
Third Edition, Print, 2011, Completely Revised.
Published in the United States of America

ISBN: 978-1-56860-149-6, eBook
ISBN: 978-1-56860-150-2, Paper
Library of Congress Control Number: 2010936666

Cataloging-in-Publication Data
Poynter, Dan.
Dan Poynter's Air Travel Handbook: by Dan Poynter. p. cm. of: Air Travel Resources. C.2011.
Includes bibliographical references.
ISBN: 978-1-56860-150-2
1. Travel, International. I. Poynter, Dan. Air Travel Handbook.
II. Title. III. Title: Air Travel Handbook. 2010936666

Table of Contents

Chapter One. On the Plane   15
   A. Flight Information
   B. Seating
   C. Food
   D. Entertainment: Reading, Listening, Viewing.
   E. Delays
   F. Safety Briefing
   G. Unpleasant Passengers and Situations

Chapter Two. Luggage & Packing   65
   A. Luggage
   B. Packing
   C. Lost Bags

Chapter Three. Health   85
   A. Vaccinations
   B. On the Plane
   C. On the Ground

Chapter Four. Security & Safety   110
   A. Security in the Airport
   B. Security on the Plane
   C. Safety off the Airport

Chapter Five. Airlines   131
   A. Airlines & Ratings
   B. Airline Alliances
   C. Loyalty Programs
   D. Airline Speak
   IATA Codes for airlines, airports, meals, time zones, etc.

Chapter Six. Air Traffic Control   176

Chapter Seven. Airports   182
   A. Airport Ratings & Statistics
   B. Club Rooms
   C. Boarding

Chapter Eight. Country Information 192
    A. Travel Statistics & Advice by Country
        Embassies
    B. People/Leaders
    C. Canada
    D. U.S.

Chapter Nine. Trip Planning 197
    A. Places to Visit
    B. Visas & Vaccination Requirments
    C. Passports
    D. Clothing
    E. Dining: Eating & Food

Chapter Ten. Borders 210
    A. Customs
    B. Immigration

Chapter Eleven. Events Around the World 215
    A. Calendars of Events.
    B. Video Conferencing vs. Being There
    C. Specific Countries

Chapter Twelve. 219
Money, Credit Cards, Exchange Rates, Fees & Taxes.
    A. Money
    B. Credit Cards
    C. Exchange Rates
    D. Fees and Taxes
    E. Tipping
    F. Airline Frequent Flyer & Hotel Stay Programs
    G. Airfares
    H Air Travel Insurance

Chapter Thirteen. 237
Communications in the air and on the road
    A. Electrical power
    B. Telephone
    C. WiFi
    D. Email

Chapter Fourteen.   249
Equipment & Technology
    A. Computers
    B. PowerPoint
    C. Batteries
    D. Public Address Systems
    E. PDAs
    F. Programs & Apps
    G. Video

Chapter Fifteen.   270
Maps, Distance Calculators & News

Chapter Sixteen. Time & Time Zones   272

Chapter Seventeen. Hotels   273

Chapter Eighteen.   292
On the Ground: Cars & Trains
    A. Automobile Renting/Hiring
    B. Train, etc. Travel

Chapter Nineteen. Expressing Yourself   298
    A. Writing about your travel
    B. Speaking about your travel

Colophon   321

Dan Speaks on air travel   322

Order Blank   323

The Air Travel Secrets are out

About the Author

As an author and professional speaker, **Dan Poynter** flies more than 6,000 miles/9,000 kms each week. He has completed 20 round-the-world itineraries, visited more than 50 countries (including skydiving into the North Pole), and spends more than 40% of his year outside the U.S. He has flown more than 2 million miles on United Airlines and has earned the coveted Global Services status (The "Black Card.")

Dan is the editor of the Global Speakers Federation *NewsBrief*, a twice-a-month newsletter on international professional speaking and travel.

Dan has been a book publisher since 1969, is the author of 127 books, and is a Certified Speaking Professional (CSP). He is a licensed pilot, FAA Master Parachute Rigger and United States Parachute Association Instructor/Examiner.

Dan studies, writes and speaks on travel, aviation, and book writing/publishing.

A Word from the Author

The *Air Travel Handbook* is about air travel. This book contains inside tips discovered by frequent flyers.

This handbook is a book of resources. I summarize each message and cite the source for the full article or web site. Rather than print information that will become dated, I lead you to websites that are kept up-to-date.

It is not a complete encyclopedia of all the lists and information on commercial flying. Instead, it contains little-known information and tips in several categories.

This is the only book on air travel written by a passenger (and licensed pilot) who has been up there. It is not a book on general travel. It is confined to air travel and it is for frequent flyers.

People have often said "Dan, you travel so much; you should write a book on air travel." My reply is always the same "Air travel changes so frequently, much would be out of date in a few weeks.

Then it came to me: an eBook is quick and easy to update. However, one limitation of the eBook format is size. Since it can't be more than 5 Mb in size, I had to remove scores of photographs. The photos have been retained for the blog but aren't included here. My apologies. See http://airtravelhandbook.com/blog/

Occasional flyers will find this book fascinating; frequent flyers will find it essential. Both will find it fun.

I hope to see you at 35,000 feet.

Acknowledgements

I am deeply indebted to friends and travel experts for their flying information and encouragement.

Howard Putnam, former CEO, Southwest Airlines and author of *The Winds of Turbulence*.

Diana Fairechild, former international chief flight attendant who flew an amazing 10 million miles.

Joe Brancatelli, Editor of JoeSentMe.com. The Home Page for Business Travelers.

Norman Zalfa, past Director of Security, ITT Europe.

Tim Gard, professional speaker on air travel and author of *Just Plane Funny*.

W Mitchell, past president of the Global Speakers Federation and author of *It's Not What Happens to You, It's What You Do About It*.

Ira Rimson, Retired Forensic Engineer specializing in aircraft accident reconstruction and analysis.

Danny O. Snow, Publishing expert and author of U-Publish.com

Maryjean Ballner, author of *Cat Massage* and *Dog Massage*. http://www.DogAndCatMassage.com

And many thanks to all the people cited in this book that contributed items, and are noted for them.

Warning—Disclaimer

This book is designed to provide information on travel. It is sold with the understanding that the publisher and author are not engaged in rendering legal, accounting, aviation, or other professional services. If legal or other expert assistance is required, the services of a competent professional should be sought.

It is not the purpose of this book to reprint all the information that is otherwise available to travelers, but instead to complement, amplify, and supplement other texts. You are urged to read all the available material, make online searches, learn as much as possible and tailor the information to your individual needs.

Every effort has been made to make this book as complete and as accurate as possible. However, there *may be mistakes*, both typographical and in content. Therefore, this text should be used only as a general guide and not as the ultimate source of information. Furthermore, this handbook contains information that is current only up to the publishing date or was available up to the publishing date.

The purpose of this handbook is to educate and entertain. The author and publisher shall have neither liability nor responsibility to any person or entity with respect to any loss or damage caused, or alleged to have been caused, directly or indirectly, by the information contained in this book.

If you do not wish to be bound by the above, you may return this book to the publisher for a full refund.

Legal Notice

Chapter One
On the Plane

A. Flight Information
B. Seating
C. Food
D. Entertainment: Reading, Listening, Viewing.
E. Delays
F. Safety Briefing
G. Unpleasant Passengers and Situations

A. Flight Information

In the U.S. the median age of flight attendants is 44. They have a much flying experience and hope they have "seen it all."

CONFIRM YOU ARE ON THE RIGHT PLANE
On entering the cabin, confirm the destination with the flight attendant at the door. "Are we going to Seattle?"

Twice, in LAX and SBA, I was among passengers sent to the wrong aircraft. Even after your boarding pass is scanned, you may be misdirected. One simple question can prevent a complex dilemma.

WHAT FLIGHT ATTENDANTS WISH PASSENGERS KNEW

The two busiest times in flight are boarding and preparing the cabin for landing. These are not good times for special requests.

Many airlines allow closing of the doors 10 minutes early, so if everyone shows up a bit early, they can depart 10 minutes early.

Do not open the galley curtain. Flight attendants need a break sometimes, and this is their break time.

Do not interrupt a flight attendant when he or she is eating.

Never touch/poke a flight attendant to get his or her attention. Use your voice or the call button.

Flight Attendants have more power than you realize. If you choose to start a fight with them, YOU WILL NOT WIN. There are laws that favor flight crews.

More fascinating advice; some you may not have heard yet.
http://bit.ly/a6UkKr

WINDOW SHADES UP FOR TAKEOFF AND LANDING

The window shades should be raised and the interior lights should be dimmed for several reasons. In the case of a crash, flight attendants and passengers will be able to see any fire or water to help them determine the best direction to evacuate. It also helps them to keep oriented—which way is up.

Post-crash, rescuers will be able to see into the cabin if the shades are up.

Dimmed cabin lighting makes the emergency-path lights on the floor easier to see.

REASONS TO DOUBLE-CHECK E-TICKETS BEFORE YOU FLY
E-ticket confirmations should be examined for some all-too-common errors.

Take a good look at names, times, seat assignments, upgrades and connections.

Print out the ticket and boarding passes. Without a hard copy, it's easy to miss details and hard to prove you are right.
http://bit.ly/9BCBhT

FLIGHT STATS
This application gives you instant access to worldwide flight status. Search by flight, route or view all airport departures and arrivals by time of day. See the websites.
http://www.flightstats.com/go/Home/home.do
http://bit.ly/90qUUO

WHY MORE FLIGHT ARE ON-TIME TODAY
Airlines have adjusted their flight arrival times to achieve a better record for on-time arrivals. That is why planes usually arrive "ahead of schedule."

BTW, Mussolini didn't really make the trains in Italy run on time, as he claimed.
http://bit.ly/hx706f

TRACK YOUR AIRLINE FLIGHT IN 3D

FBOweb has an application that works in conjunction with Google Earth to show the flight path of a selected flight over a virtual landscape, all in real time. There's a detailed review at
http://bit.ly/9RTofT

AIRLINE PASSENGER BUMPING ON THE RISE IN US

U.S. airlines are denying boarding to the most passengers in nine years as business travelers resume flying following the deepest cuts in seats since World War II.

Almost 220,000 passengers couldn't get on their ticketed flights in the first quarter; this is 25 percent more than a year earlier.

Bumping rates will not improve until airlines increase capacity.

Check-in and get your boarding passes online 24 hours prior to departure and get to the airport early.
http://bit.ly/bf5X4Z

TICKET ABBREVIATIONS DICTATE WHO GETS BUMPED

Embedded in the letters and numbers on your airline ticket (not boarding pass) is a letter-code that lets airline personnel know what kind of passenger you are and what you paid for your ticket. They can use these to quickly determine whether you should be the first or the last to get bumped, and whether you can get a seat upgrade. See the detailed booking classes.

First Class: F, A, P, R.
Business Class: C, J, D, I, Z.
Economy/Coach class: Y, B, M, H, G, K, L, N, O, Q, S, T, U, V, W, X.
A lowercase "n" after any class code indicates Night Service.
http://en.wikipedia.org/wiki/Travel_class
http://bit.ly/djyjXt

TURBULENCE
Rough air is called "chop" and can happen at any time. Massive updrafts may cause the plane to bump up and down quickly.

Keep the seatbelt fastened whenever you are in your seat. When the chop is particularly rough, the pilot will slow the speed of the plane to reduce forces on the airframe.

Pilots try to avoid turbulence not because they're afraid a wing is going to rip off but because it's chop is aggravating. The plane is designed to take the bumps.

The smoothest rides are in the middle of the plane, over the wing. Think of a seesaw: the ends move up and down more than the middle.

Smoother flights usually occur in the morning. As the ground heats up, thermals (heated, rising air) are caused and result in "bumpier air." Thunderstorms are more likely in the afternoon.

When in the lavatory, hang on to the handle and/or brace yourself against the ceiling. You never know when chop can occur. If the air becomes rough while in the lavatory, close the toilet lid to guard against splash.

> The strength of the turbulence is directly proportional to the temperature of your coffee.
> — *Gunter's Second Law of Air Travel*

AIRLINE PILOT EXPLAINS AIR TURBULENCE
Video. http://bit.ly/gNGQRW

WHEN NOT TO FLY
Holiday travel advice in video from Peter Greenberg. http://bit.ly/fl4jPY

HOW TO THANK A PILOT
Most of the time, how you land a plane is a good indicator of a pilot's skill. So if you want to say something appreciative to a pilot as you're getting off the plane, say "Smooth landing." Pilots appreciate that.

B. Seating

First Class, Business Class, and Sardine Class.

FACTOID
Reclining seat issues account for some 75% of the in-flight disputes.

SEAT NUMBERING
On most aircraft, seats are numbered across A, B, C, D, E, F, G, H, J, L; more seats per row on a widebody.
Note that the letter I is missing; that is to avoid confusion with number 1. A is a window seat on the port side.

CHANGING SEATS
To find a better location in your cabin, go online or call the airline just past midnight on the day of flight. Unpaid reservations may be cancelled, freeing some reserved seats. Ask again at check-in and at the gate. Keep asking at each point.
If you do not ask, the answer is "no."

GLOSSARY OF AIRPLANE SEATING TERMS
Become an expert or, at least, sound like one. For example:

> **FEBO**: An acronym to help you remember that American Airlines serves its first class customers from the **F**ront on **E**ven numbered flights and from the **B**ack on **O**dd numbered flights. Being served first usually results in getting your choice of meals.
>
> **Op-Up**: An "Operational Upgrade" occurs when the Economy section of the plane is oversold, but there are seats available in a

premium class, and the airline gate agent will be forced to move an Economy passenger to the premium cabin. This is basically a "free" upgrade.

Stationary Armrest: An armrest (seat divider) that does not lift. Typically found on the aisle, or when a tray table is located inside the armrest at a bulkhead

See more seating terms at
http://www.seatguru.com/glossary.php

FEWER AIRLINE UPGRADES PREDICTED
Y-UP and Q-UP fares go to those flyers that pay. See http://bit.ly/cbxI9q

"SEAT PITCH"
Seat pitch refers to the distance between the same locations on two seats and is expressed in inches. It measures the space occupied by the seat plus its legroom.

BOOKING THE BEST SEAT
More than just price, pitch, amenities, and availability.

Sitting near the engines may be noisier, near the exit row may be safer in case of an evacuation, and near the back is usually bumpier during turbulence.
http://bit.ly/bzWO3G
http://seatexpert.com/, http://bit.ly/bMsUyD

HOW TO PICK A GREAT AIRLINE SEAT
See the video at
http://bit.ly/gKMkzd

SECRET SEATS ON PLANES
--Peter Greenberg, USA.

You can get better seats even in Coach. See the video at
http://bit.ly/dS5Hec

BUSINESS AND FIRST CLASS GET MORE THAN BETTER SEATS

a. Wines. The more expensive wines are served up front and the airlines buy them tax-free.

For example, in First Class, Singapore Air serves a Burgundy: Bouchard Le Corton, 2006, costing $100 USD a bottle.

The red wine is always ice cold because of a U.S. Food and Drug Administration rule that all food be kept at 40F/4C for at least 12 hours before a fight.

Letite Teague of *The Wall Street Journal* said: "I'd also reached a few class-specific conclusions: I'd fly Singapore for first class, United for business and I'd be happy on Air New Zealand drinking in coach.
http://bit.ly/cyt16b

b. Hotels. If there is a long equipment delay, the airlines will lodge the passengers overnight. First

Class passenger are often sent to **** or ***** hotels while Economy passengers sleep under fewer stars.

BOARD EARLY
Not only will you have your choice of overhead space, there is less risk to being reseated (to a middle seat in the rear of the plane) to accommodate a couple that wants to sit together or a mother who needs to be near her children. It is not your fault that some people book late and fail to plan ahead.

STOW YOUR BAGS PROPERLY
When overhead space is scarce, some passengers will place a bag in the compartment with most of it sticking out. They leave the problem to the flight attendant. They risk having their bag removed and placed in the very rear of the cabin or gate checked. And they may not even know where it has been stowed.

By the way, it's against FAA regulations for a flight attendant to shut an aircraft door until all the overhead bins have been closed.
http://bit.ly/aAcEkh

AIRLINES--MORE SEATS AVAILABLE UP FRONT
Flights within Central America, between Africa and the Far East, and across the Pacific have the most vacant premium seats.
http://bit.ly/abKNFm, http://bit.ly/aL9yTE

SEAT UPGRADES ON STAR ALLIANCE PARTNER AIRLINES

Asking your primary or Alliance airline for an upgrade to Business or First using miles, usually results in a run-around or denial.

If on one or more routes, you are flying All Nippon, United, Lufthansa, Asiana, ANA, Austrian, LOT-Polish, SWISS, TAP Portugal or Thai Airways, your seating is upgradable with miles.

Try this website first:
http://bit.ly/d8QRtH

CHECK ON AIRCRAFT SEATING WITH YOUR PDA OR SMART PHONE.

Mobile SeatGuru is a version of the website optimized for handheld devices. All you need is a device with an HTML-capable (Internet) browser such as the iPhone, BlackBerry 7000 series, TREO, Dell Axim, HP iPAQ, Pocket PCs, Mac, PC, or various advanced mobile phones.

This service is free! From your PDA or phone, go to http://mobile.seatguru.com and see
http://www.seatguru.com/articles/mobile_launch.php
http://seatexpert.com/

THE PROs & CONs OF BULKHEAD SEATING

Pros: Usually there is more legroom in the first rows, it is easier to get out of a window seat, and there is no seat in front of you that could recline into your space.

Cons: The armrests in the bulkhead seats often are not moveable because they must support tables. And there is no seat in front of you to store a bag under. See http://bit.ly/fQyHoJ

RAISING THE ARMREST

Armrests between the seats in Economy can be raised but aisle armrests are usually latched down.

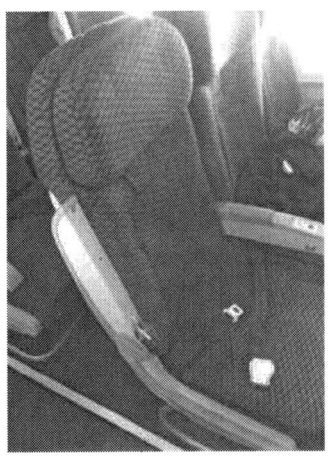

Search under and around the armrest for a button or latch to release the armrest so you can swing it up.

If the armrest is ridged, it can't be raised. If wobbles, it is probably hinged.

Now you may raise the armrest, swing your legs into the aisle and stand up without raising your tray table.

NEW "SADDLE CLASS" STAND-UP SEATING

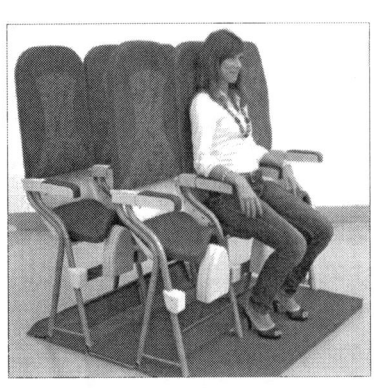

Saddle Class brings a whole new meaning to the term "cattle class," a plane seat that is shaped like a saddle and could allow airlines to squeeze in even more passengers.

Named the 'Skyrider,' the new seat design

promises to attract plenty of attention from airlines hoping to increase the number of seats in the Economy Class sections of planes, presumably without compromising on comfort.

Passengers sit at an angle with just 23"/58 cm of legroom between them and the seat in front - a whopping 7"/28 cm less than the current average seat pitch of around 30"/76 cm. This sort of seat is only suitable for a passenger of about 5ft 10in. If you are shorter your legs won't reach the floor and if you are taller your legs stretch out in the aisle. These seats may not accommodate some skirts and dresses.

Read more:
http://bit.ly/c6tHEe, http://bit.ly/ajUYmw

And for more seating ideas, see http://aol.it/g57oWw

EXIT-ROW SEATS
The seats in the Exit Row usually have more legroom to allow easier access to the exit door. The seats in the row in from of the exit row often do not recline—again to provide more exit room.

Passengers seated in the Exit Row must verbally agree to assist the crew in an evacuation and must not be very young.

In case of an emergency, you will be closer to the exit. And you will find it easier to locate the exit in a smoky cabin.

CUDDLE CLASS

Some airlines are starting to introduce rows of three economy class seats together that can be converted into a large, flat space suitable for families or couples who want to stretch out next to each other. Two passengers travelling together will be able to book the third seat in the row for half price.

The seats, known as "Skycouches" and light-heartedly referred to as "cuddle class", have been earmarked for launch on some Air New Zealand services from Auckland to Los Angeles.
http://bit.ly/c0E1YT

SEATING WHEN YOU ARE TRAVELING WITH A PARTNER

Flying with your significant other and want more room—together?
Some couples are successful booking a window seat and an aisle seat.

If no one is assigned the middle seat, you will get all three seats. If someone does show up for the middle seat, ask if he or she would prefer to seat next to the window or an aisle. Then, at least, you two can sit together. Worth trying.

Another alternative to consider: book aisle seats-- across from each other.

POWER TO THE SEATS
Which aircraft supply electrical power for passenger use? Is it 110v AC or 15v DC? How many watts? Enough for that power-hungry laptop with the 17" screen and DVD player? Should you buy a power adapter or an extra battery? See:
http://bit.ly/aRlYpt

AIRLINE SEAT-EXIT ETIQUETTE
When getting up from your airline seat, do not assist yourself by grabbing the seatback in front of you. Its occupant can feel your jostling the seat. This is especially annoying when the occupant is trying to sleep.

Tuck your feet under you and push down on your armrests. While somewhat awkward, it is more considerate to support yourself using your own seat.

Exceptions are some of the newer "suite seats" in business and first class that are standalone. Many have edges you can grab to assist your standing up. Some have grab handles.

RECLINING YOUR SEAT
Ease your seat back slowly. Do not startle the person seated behind you and do not disturb their tray. Reclining seats have broken many laptop computers.

FLYING ETIQUETTE
What considerate passengers do.
Top ten lists.
http://www.airportcitycodes.com/topten.html
http://www.airportcitycodes.com/toptenun.html
http://www.airportcitycodes.com/toptengood.html

WHEN A FLIGHT ATTENDANT ADVISES YOU THE SEATBELT SIGN IS ON

You may just acknowledge the crewmember and continue to the lavatory. Don't ask the flight attendant if you *may* go. They are required to *advise* you to be seated not to *prohibit* your mission.

Sometimes the Fasten Seat Belt lights are switched on for the benefit of the crew. It is hard to serve from carts when passengers want to get by for the lavatory.

On the other hand, when the pilot tells the crew to sit down, the flight may be dangerously rough. Sit down and buckle up.

Listen to the seatbelt briefing when belt light goes on. It usually says the flight attendants are here to *advise* you.

See the explanation at
http://www.airline-advisor.com/TB/?P=4726

TALL TRAVELERS

Some will argue that people can avoid being overweight but they do not choose being tall. Commercial airliners and their seats are not designed for tall people.

The FAA does require passengers be able to sit belted and with both armrests down to comply with safety standards, so most carriers now have policies on travelers who are too obese to fit into one seat.

Many airlines require fliers who spill over into their neighbor's space to buy a second ticket, which may or may not be refunded later.

But tall passengers without weight issues generally have no trouble with the horizontal dimensions of a coach seat.

If you are more than 6'/2m tall, try asking for an exit row or bulkhead seat. Get a note from your doctor requesting more legroom. Stand up straight and show your height at check-in and at the gate.

The greatest challenge for tall men will be the lavatory. The ceiling is low and the facing bulkhead is curved toward you requiring you to lean back. You can't see what is going on below.

The toilets on the Boeing 737 aircraft are the greatest challenge. Even after 9,000+ aircraft and all these years of service, these popular aircraft still do not come equipped with toilet seats that will stay up.

It may be impossible for a tall man to hold up the seat.

Request pre-boarding so that you can find room in the overhead bins for your luggage. You need the room under the seat in front of you for your legs.
http://www.cnn.com/2010/TRAVEL/10/14/tall.fliers.rant/

Some airlines are charging for extra legroom.
http://www.ecademy.com/node.php?id=136259

Make an online search and read up on "Knee Defender"

See the Tall Persons Club web site and its travel resources.
http://www.tallclub.co.uk/netresources/index.asp

GETTING LEGROOM ON "NO FRILLS" PLANES
--Alan Stevens, UK. *The Tall Traveler.*

A few days ago, I flew from London to Seville on one of Ryanair's new planes. One great innovation for tall travelers is that the seats don't recline - so that there is no chance of having your patella crushed by the person in front. However, the seat pitch is not great, so I was still uncomfortable in the standard seats. However, the two rows of central emergency exit seats have masses of room, and were ideal--so we shifted into them as soon as we spotted a couple of empty ones.

The problem with low-cost airlines is that there is no seat allocation, and therefore no chance of pre-booking the emergency exit seats. However, they do now have a policy of giving you a number at check-in, and then boarding the plane in two groups (e.g. numbers under 51 first). So you need to arrive early to get into the first group. If the plane is boarding by both front and rear doors, aim for the rear one. The first group of people will be going up the front steps for seats near the front, and probably will have blocked the gangways, preventing people from reaching the middle of the plane.

If you have a small child with you, you can often board first, but of course the children can't sit in the emergency exit seats. If your partner is with you, they can sit in the row behind (or in front). OK, you won't be sitting beside them, but that's a small price to pay for comfort!
http://thetalltraveller.blogspot.com/ , http://bit.ly/e8rjkC

✈ BLOG FOR THE TALL TRAVELER
--Alan Stevens, UK. *The Tall Traveler*.

There must be millions of us who can't get enough leg room on planes, have to crouch under hotel showers, or find that beds are way too short.

This blog has been years in the making. I have visited dozens of countries, thousands of hotels and made countless plane trips. I'd like to gather and share experiences of tall travelers like me, so that everyone's life could be a little more comfortable. And that's what we all want, isn't it?

So how tall is tall? Well, I'm six foot three (around 192 cm, I think), and see plenty of people as tall or taller than I am (especially in The Netherlands). http://thetalltraveller.blogspot.com/

MAGAZINES: LESS WEIGHT = LESS FUEL COSTS
Many airlines have eliminated carrying magazines (except for their own.) This is another way to save weight.
http://www.youtube.com/watch?v=EvbK17MgJXg

AIRLINES WILL NOT CUT BACK ON THEIR OWN MAGAZINES
The glossy airline magazines will likely survive the fuel-related financial downsizing.

That's because there is still enough advertising to keep the magazines profitable. And the well-heeled passengers who read them still love them--spending an average of 26 minutes per issue,
http://bit.ly/bxP7xb

HOW AIRLINE MAGAZINES OPERATE
Magazine publishers bear all the costs of producing the magazines and pay airlines an amount tied to passenger traffic and the carriers' markets. The publisher, in turn, gets the revenue that comes from selling ads.
http://bit.ly/cDxDvM

FLYING WITH BABIES
Everything on a plane, including coffeepots, has to be restrained during takeoff and landing and in

times of turbulence. In the case of a baby, the parent or guardian is their seat belt.

According to government estimates, more than 7-million children under the age of two fly on parents' laps on U.S. carriers each year. You are not required to purchase a seat for your baby until he or she turns two and airlines don't charge for families to check a car seat. That is the crux of the issue that has stymied safety experts and pediatricians for years and has perhaps lulled parents into a false sense of security. Flight attendants may refer to these babies as "Lap Children."

It is up to you whether you want to protect your baby in a car seat.
http://bit.ly/9StW9h
http://bit.ly/bvvB0T

Do you really want to hold the baby in your lap for the entire flight? Do you want you baby to become a projectile in rough air?

The Baby B'Air Flight Vest® secures your child to your lap belt to protect against the unexpected dangers of turbulence and to keep your child safely on your lap during flight.
http://www.babybair.com/

Children who drop off to sleep at the sound of a car's engine are likely to be lulled off by the plane's engine.

Babies less than 12 weeks old may suffer more from pressure variations due to smaller-diameter Eustachian tubes and under-developed lungs.

Babies given something to suck or swallow may be less bothered by pressure changes during ascent and descent.
http://www.faa.gov/passengers/fly%5Fchildren/crs/
http://on.msnbc.com/eSXXIl

FLYING WITH CHILDREN
Keeping them entertained, quiet and safe.
Avoid placing a child in an aisle seat. A wheeled cart could crush a small hand. Most youngsters will prefer a window seat anyway.

More tips.
http://bit.ly/hXXmIz

CHILDREN FLYING ALONE
"UMs" (unaccompanied minors).

Thinking about letting your child fly alone? Make sure you check with your airline before you buy your ticket. Most airlines allow a child under the age of 18 to fly alone, and the rules and restrictions for what they call unaccompanied children are different for each airline. Airlines are free to enforce any rules they want, and no two airlines have exactly the same polices.

Nonstop flights will avoid confusing plane changes. Identify the person picking up your child, don't book evening flights that could leave the child stranded,

make sure he or she has a mobile phone, do not leave the airport until the flight is off the ground, etc.
http://www.airsafe.com/kidsafe/kidrules.htm
http://bit.ly/flkxlH

FLYING WITH PETS
More than half a million animals travel by air in the U.S. each year.

Check each airline website for rules and charges. Consider container requirements, acclimation, veterinary certificates, temperature restrictions, etc.

For example: United Airlines accepts dogs, cats, birds, rabbits, hamsters and guinea pigs as checked baggage. Birds including parrots, cocktails and ferrets are accepted in the cargo area, whether or not you are on the same flight. Small dogs and cats more than 8 weeks old and household birds that fit comfortably in carriers underneath the seat in front of you, are accepted as carry-on.

For airline requirements, details, documents, and pet carriers, see
http://www.FlyGOB.com
http://www.pettravel.com/airline_rules.cfm
http://bit.ly/cIHYIP

SECURITY SCREENING AND DIABETIES SUPPLIES
Diabetic patients planning to travel by air can eliminate the chaotic screening situation by being aware of the recommendations by Transportation Security Administration (TSA). It is wise that

passengers with diabetes inform the screening authorities about the medical conditions and the supplies they need to carry along during the travel. Though not required by TSA, better carry the prescription label to fasten the screening process.
http://ezinearticles.com/?Air-Travel-Tips-for-Diabetic-Patients&id=5509745

AIR TRAVEL WITH A SERVICE ANIMAL
Advice from Guide Dogs for the Blind
http://www.sandiego.org/article/Visitors/1767

C. Food

FACTOID
Today, passengers drink more bottled water on board than sodas.

The Captain and First Officer eat different meals in case the food should make one of them sick.

Tolerance for alcohol drops with the reduction in pressure. Airlines are pressurized to around 8,000-feet/2438 m. Drink less for the same alcoholic effect.

THE MANIFEST CONTROLS WHO GET SERVED FIRST
A manifest is printed for each flight. Among other things, it includes the rank of the passengers. In First Class, rank determines the order for when each passenger is asked his or her meal choice.

For example, on United, there is a manifest section titled

CUSTOMER STATUS LEVEL FOR MEALS
1. **** - GS (Global Services)
2. *** - 1K / FULL FARE CUSTOMERS – ALL STATUS
3. ** - PREMIER EXEC / EXEC MILLION / STAR ALLIANCE*GOLD
4. * - PREMIER / STAR ALLIANCE* SILVER

As a courtesy, the high-ranking passenger's seatmate is usually asked his or her preference regardless of rank. An assumption is made you are traveling together. Even sitting next to a Global Services member has it perks.

HOW AIRLINE MEALS ARE MADE
See what is involved in the planning and preparation of a large number of airline meals. Video.
http://www.youtube.com/watch?v=alh_2xg5GWo

IN-FLIGHT FOOD TRIES TO BE TASTY
When airlines gave away food, the motivation was to minimize cost. Now that most airlines are selling food, they have an incentive to provide better choice and quality to passengers.
http://nyti.ms/bC9CaI

FOR BETTER AIRLINE FOOD
Order a "special meal."
Carbohydrates may help you deal with less oxygen.
http://www.Flyana.com/
http://www.heraldnet.com/article/20080106/LIVING05/733641941

NOISE MAY AFFECT THE TASTE OF AIRLINE FOOD

A study found that high levels of background noise could make people's taste palates less sensitive. So your meal may taste bland because of the roar of the engines.

On the other hand, pleasant sounds may make food taste better.
http://bit.ly/92JSw1

D. Entertainment: Reading, listening, viewing.

eBOOK READER FOR YOUR PDA OR MOBILE PHONE

Frequent travelers spend a lot of time in airports and on planes. Waiting time can be a benefit; it gives us time to read.

Whatever electronic communication device you are carrying, there is a book reader for it: iPhone, iPad, Nook, Pocket PC, PalmOs, Windows Mobile, Symbian (Series 60, Series 80, 90, UIQ), Blackberry, Franklin, iLiad (by iRex), BenQ-Siemens or Pepper Pad.

And if you have a Symbian Smartphone, a Franklin, an iLiad, a BenQ-Siemens or a Pepper Pad, there is a good chance that Mobipocket Reader (Kindle) is already installed!

To download the Reader software, see http://bit.ly/aqDA66

eBooks may be downloaded from Amazon.com, BarnesAndNoble.com, Mobipocket.com, Fictionwise.com, and other sites.

AMAZON KINDLE eBOOKS CAN BE READ ON OTHER DEVICES.

You do not need a Kindle to read Kindle books. You can read them on PCs, Macs, iPhones, BlackBerrys, iPADs, Androids, and others.

Download the free software at
http://amzn.to/aIYVXq

READING & LISTENING TO PRINTED BOOKS ON THE PLANE

An inexpensive way to purchase books.

Purchase your books at Amazon.com—used. Most are just a few dollars plus $3.95 shipping. In most cases, you will only read the book once and then discard it. If you do not intend to keep/display the books, why pay new prices?

Then recycle the books by leaving them in the waiting area at an airport. Pass them on. Some travelers like to write on the cover: "Please take and read this book. Then leave it in an airport for the next traveler."

Also, purchase your audiobooks at Amazon—used. Only 5% or so are not in their original shrinkwrap; they are unused. Why pay $45 for an audiobook when you can get one for around $12?

E. Delays

AIRLINE GLITCHES ARE TOP CAUSES OF FLIGHT DELAYS
Airline problems, such as pilot shortages, taking too long to refuel and mechanical breakdowns ("mechanicals"), are as much at the root of delays as bad weather (WX) and heavy air traffic (ATC).
http://bit.ly/cakvl3

FLIGHT DELAY TRACKER
http://usat.ly/eYbvah

STRANDED AT THE AIRPORT?
Don't Forget Rule 240

Rule 240 originally stated that in the event of a cancellation or flight misconnection, the airline would have to put you on their next flight out, or, if that wasn't "acceptable," on the next flight out of a competing airline if that flight would get you to your destination sooner, all at no additional cost to you. If only first class was available on the other airline, then they had to upgrade you. This only applied in circumstances under the airlines' control, such as crew failing to show up, or mechanical problems.

Legacy airlines in the U.S., such as United, American, US Air, and Delta, still honor the old CAB Rule but you have to ask. Each carrier has changed the wording in its Contract of Carriage with United being the most generous. See
http://www.msnbc.msn.com/id/22900119/
http://bit.ly/cKoLXx

http://bit.ly/e8vJ57
http://bit.ly/dXpi8R

Peter Greenberg shares some tips on how to know if your flight is truly delayed. Plus he provides an insider tip on Rule 240.
http://www.youtube.com/watch?v=CT-SWdvL2KY

You'll be sure to get on your way sooner than other passengers that aren't aware of Rule 240. See the video.
http://www.youtube.com/watch?v=ze4twPrvH14

AIRLINE CONDITIONS OF CARRIAGE
Your ticket and the Conditions of Carriage constitute the contract between you, the passenger, and the airline. Here are links to them.

Alitalia
http://bit.ly/cQHoPv

American.
http://bit.ly/a7m3Zr

Delta
http://bit.ly/dQEf6t

Jet Blue
http://www.jetblue.com/p/jetblue_coc.pdf

Lufthansa
http://bit.ly/dAOCjr

Singapore Air
http://bit.ly/beHB4p

United
http://bit.ly/hBfHY8

US Air
http://bit.ly/bbcpdP

HOW TO ESCAPE DOWN AN AIRPLANE SLIDE
--Tom Stoyan, Canada's Sales Coach.

Emergency airplane evacuations happen more often than most people think; about once every 11 days in the U.S.

Suggestions for a quick and successful evacuation: Plan ahead, move quickly, jump, keep your heels up, and your arms crossed over your chest, and move away from the bottom of the slide.
http://bit.ly/e0xbS3

THE THREE-HOUR RULE
Cabin Fever?

New U.S. rules force airlines to get passengers off planes after 3 hours on the ground or face heavy fines.

See the YouTube report:
http://bit.ly/bTamty

HOW TO GET OFF THE PLANE
Sooner than the three-hour rule

Some people have tried to get off earlier by declaring sickness. They claim the airline must respond to a medical emergency. This is not recommended, as there could be repercussions.

F. Safety Briefings
Why is it the safety briefing before the flight is loud and clear but the rest of the announcements in flight are difficult to understand?

WHY YOU ARE REQUESTED TO STOW COMPUTERS, iPods, ETC.

Computers should be stowed for takeoff and landing so they do not become projectiles in a crash landing.

iPods should be turned off so you can hear instructions during the emergency briefing and during an emergency while taking off or landing. See http://dir.salon.com/topics/ask_the_pilot/

SAFETY BRIEFING (WARNING) FROM A PILOT
--Beth Terry, USA.
Video.
http://www.youtube.com/watch?v=reRRgEET6Kw

DRINKING ALCOHOL AND SAFETY
Passengers may drink alcohol during flight but should not be drunk as they may not respond properly during an emergency.

G. Unpleasant Passengers & Situations

Some people create unpleasant flying situations. You may have encountered some of them Those who perform personal acts such as clipping their toenails, do not bring diapers for their babies, do not have a pen to fill out the immigration forms for other countries, and so on.

> "I have found that there ain't no surer way to find out whether you like people or hate them than to travel with them."
> **--Mark Twain.**

AIRPLANE URBAN LEGENDS DEBUNKED
Is lightning dangerous to airplanes (no).
Will toilets on plane suck you into them (no).
Will breast implants explode with reduced air pressure (no).
http://bit.ly/aoOLiX

PASSENGERS BEHAVING BADLY
Rude neighbors and messes left in seat pockets proliferate.

Exploring the revenge motive. See
http://bit.ly/bspWcx

THE DEADLY SINS OF MIDDLE SEATMATES
Ever get trapped next to that traveler who thinks your shoulder is a pillow? And other things inconsiderate passengers do to make your flight miserable.
http://bit.ly/cv2cKU

BSGs TO PAY MORE FOR AIRLINE SEATS

On United flights, larger passengers who need a seatbelt extender in order to buckle up or who cannot get the armrests down around themselves must now either purchase an extra seat, upgrade to business or first class or wait for the next flight.

Tim Gard, humor speaker, describes a major flying fear: being seated next to the **Big Sweaty Guy** (BSG).

Airlines are charging for "extra" services. It costs more to check a bag, to board early (to have access to overhead space), and to speak with a human who can make your travel plans and explain fare rules. Perhaps they can charge to guarantee a seat next to a smaller person, not the BSG.

"RUDENESS POLL"
Reveals what really annoys passengers

Loud, foul-mouthed seatmates and rushing to exit at the end of a flight are among passengers' top complaints about their fellow travelers.
http://bit.ly/aCj6YE
YouTube video. Humor.
http://www.youtube.com/watch?v=B7FNUx3rnW8

INSIDE BUSINESS TRAVEL SURVEY REVEALS THE REALITY OF BUSINESS TRAVEL TODAY

It may come as no surprise to modern-day road warriors, but "last-minute flight cancellations and delays" are the biggest gripe of today's international business traveler. The survey also found that hotel-

bound business travelers remain frustrated by basic inconveniences. See
http://bit.ly/dmd2vQ

GUARD YOUR CARRY-ONS
Items can be removed from your seat-back pocket, purse or luggage while you sleep or are in the lavatory. Some flight attendants have been known to steal valuables. Air France had reports of 142 thefts in one six-month period. Japanese businessmen are a known target; they often carry large amounts of cash, credit cards, and valuables. If possible, lock the pockets of your bags carrying valuables. **Or, carry your valuables in a "fanny pack."**

TEMPERATURE OF THE CABIN
You are sitting in the cabin and are cold. The flight attendants are bustling around and are warm. They may not realize the cabin is cold. Ask one to call the captain and request an increase the cabin temperature.

SMOKING: MANY STILL LIGHT UP ON PLANES
Passengers are caught smoking on U.S. airliners at least twice a week. The Federal Aviation Administration has brought 696 cases, some for civil fines of thousands of dollars, against people caught smoking aboard airliners in the past five years. Lighting a cigarette on a plane has been banned for 20 years.
http://bit.ly/c5OpDk

SOME AIRLINE STOWAWAYS ARE DISGUSTING

Mice, mosquitoes, scorpions, maggots, and other small insects can breeze past airport security, and they do not seem to mind flying in First Class or in Coach.

Passengers on a US Airways flight were disgusted to find maggots falling on them from an overhead bin. Pilots declared an emergency and returned to the gate in Atlanta at Hartsfield-Jackson International Airport.

The extensive security process may leave passengers feeling that their bodies and possessions are thoroughly inspected before boarding, but there are no regulations prohibiting passengers from bringing rotting meat on a plane, which is apparently how the maggots got onto the jetliner.

Rodents are especially challenging because they gnaw and jump. In January 2008, eight mice were found on a United Airlines plane in China.

See the full article at
http://nyti.ms/hYFtOg

EQUIPMENT PROBLEMS
--Dan Poynter, USA.

Your plane may have an equipment malfunction and have to return to the originating airport or land at another one. As this is a carrier problem, the airline will often pay for your hotel, meals, etc. Sometimes the plane is repaired and takes off after the delay and sometimes you are put on another flight.

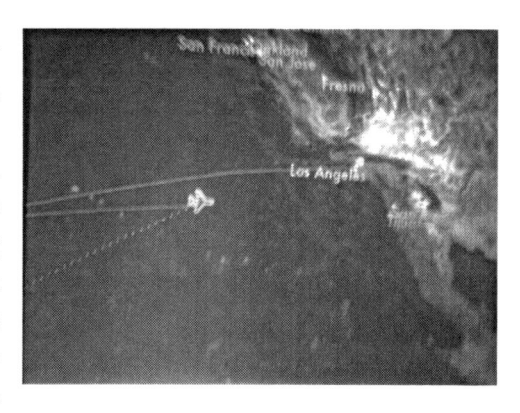

Ask what your choices are.
I was on a United flight from LAX to SYD. Four hours into the fight, the cabin heater was malfunctioning so we returned to LAX. See the unusual photo of the flight-tracking map on the seat-back monitor. The plane was repaired and we took of again 24 hours later.

FLIGHT ATTENDANT QUITS. MAKES DRAMATIC EXIT.
Crewmembers can be affected by air rage

As the JetBlue plane was landing at JFK, a passenger got up to retrieve a bag from the overhead bin. Flight attendant Steven Slater instructed the person to remain seated. The passenger defied him.

Mr. Slater reached the passenger just as the luggage was coming down; it struck Mr. Slater in the head. Slater asked for an apology. Instead, the passenger cursed him.

Slater grabbed the microphone and said, "To the passenger who called me a M*@#&% -- F*&% you. I've been in the business 28 years. I've had it. He grabbed two beers, activated, and slid down the emergency inflatable slide, and went home.

Some of the passengers sided with the flight attendant. http://bit.ly/a1fVQX

PLAYMATE ATTEMPTS TO OPEN DOOR IN FLIGHT
Playmate Tiffany Livingston was detained after she reportedly tried to open the door of an airplane mid-flight in September 2010. The 21-year-old was arrested and placed in federal custody. She was a centerfold in VIP, the Singapore edition of *Playboy*. http://bit.ly/aYqqaU

REMOVING LINT DURING FLIGHT
The airline blanket left lint on your black clothing and you do not have a lint roller. What to do? Check the drawers in the lavatory for sanitary napkin pads. They have an adhesive area. Just strip off the cover strip and use the napkin for a lint pick-up.

IS JIM WILSON ON YOUR FLIGHT?
"Jim Wilson" is the name often given to a dead passenger being transported in the cargo area.

Peter Greenberg reveals who may be riding with you—and where.
http://www.youtube.com/watch?v=IByMYHswzEI

PASSENGERS AND TERRORISTS
--Dan Poynter, USA.

Passengers have been instrumental in foiling most terrorist attempts on airliners.
Here is an idea that has been submitted to the TSA to educate passengers as to what they can do.

(Proposed card for commercial airliner seat-back pockets)

A Message to Passengers From the Transportation Safety Administration

and the

Federal Aviation Administration

Instructions

Watch the passengers around you.

✈ If another passenger is acting suspiciously

Air Travel Handbook, Page 53 of 322

🏠 Ring the Call Button above your seat to summon the fight attendants.

✈ **If you see anyone lighting a match**, etc.

🗣 Yell FIRE!
    Yelling will alert nearby passengers.

🕯 Put out the fire.

🏠 Ring the Call Button to summon the flight attendants.

👁 Restrain the perpetrator.

See other side of this card for explanations

**A Message to Passengers
From the
Transportation Safety Administration**

and the

Federal Aviation Administration

Explanation

You are the first line of defense against airline hijackers and bombers.
Flight attendants cannot watch the activities of every passenger on this aircraft.
Nor can Air Marshals, when they are aboard.
But *you* can watch the passengers around you.

So far, only two terrorists have tried to blow up airliners in flight. In each case, they were identified and restrained by nearby passengers.

We are not asking you to be an "Air Marshall," nor are we asking you to "spy" but you can alert flight attendants if you see suspicious activity. Simply follow the instructions on the reverse of this card.

You can delay the bomber until professional help arrives.

See other side of this card for steps on how you can help.

The above suggestion has not been accepted by any governmental body. It is presented by Dan Poytner for discussion.

iPODS & iPHONES ON PLANES
Following in Singapore Air's footsteps as "the world's largest flying iPod dock," United announced that it

would become the first U.S. airline to offer in-flight iPod and iPhone entertainment system connectivity.

United Airlines is giving passengers the option of plugging their iPod or iPhone into their seat's entertainment console to watch videos on their personal 15.4-inch screen--and all while the device charges.
http://bit.ly/fLr2Mn, http://gizmo.do/ceERAe

US GOVERNMENT REGULATIONS PROTECTING CONSUMERS
Here are the consumer protection rules from the Department of Transportation (DOT).
http://airconsumer.dot.gov/publications/flyrights.htm

☺ Humor

WHEN WILL WE CRASH?

On a flight home, I was upgraded to First Class.
The passenger in the adjacent seat was in uniform—a pilot. What an opportunity to ask questions about aviation.

He patiently answered my questions about the airline industry, work schedules, the food served in each cabin, what they do with unruly passengers, what makes rough flying, why can't they avoid rough weather, how many crew are up front, why airports are sometimes short of gates, and so on.

Finally, I got around to flying emergencies.

Q: "What happens if an engine fails?
A: This plane is designed to fly on just one engine so we continue with the other one.

Q: If the other engine fails, how long until we hit the ground?
A: The pilot looked at me in perfect deadpan and answered:
"The rest of your life."

CLASSES OF AIR TRAVEL
"There are two classes of travel:
First Class and with children."
--Robert Benchley, humorist.

WHAT WAS THE PROBLEM?
Taxiing down the tarmac, the jetliner abruptly stopped, turned around and returned to the gate.

After an hour-long wait, it finally took off.
A concerned passenger asked the flight attendant, "What was the problem?"

"The pilot was bothered by a noise he heard in the engine," explained the flight attendant, "and it took us a while to find a new pilot."

OBNOXIOUS AIRLINE PASSENGERS:
Video from Princess Cruises.
http://www.youtube.com/watch?v=dSOdXpndCIo

CEBU PACIFIC AIRLINES DANCING FLIGHT ATTENDENTS
Female flight attendants dance and sing. Videos.

http://www.youtube.com/watch?v=2SBL6dgBBak
And the male flight attendants too.
http://www.youtube.com/watch?v=40O0lROkLWI

PILLOW FIGHT BREAKS OUT ON PLANE
All-around fun! A pillow fight broke out on a Lufthansa flight and a passenger caught it on video. The entire coach cabin was involved and massive cheering broke out after it was done. Video.
http://www.youtube.com/watch?v=rwDlHJCRCjg

FUNNY STEWARD RAPPING SAFETY INFORMATION ON SOUTHWEST AIRLINES
Video. http://bit.ly/eKyoic

FLIGHT ATTENDANT ANNOUNCEMENTS
"Thank you for flying Delta Business Express. We hope you enjoyed giving us the business as much as we enjoyed taking you for a ride."

"There may be 50 ways to leave your lover, but there are only 4 ways out of this airplane..."

"Your seat cushions can be used for flotation, and in the event of an emergency water landing, please take them with our compliments."

"We'd like to thank you folks for flying with us today. And, the next time you get the insane urge to go blasting through the skies in a pressurized metal tube, we hope you'll think of us here at US Airways."
"Weather at our destination is 20 degrees with some broken clouds, but they'll try to have them fixed before we arrive. Thank you, and remember, nobody

loves you, or your money, more than Southwest Airlines."

"Last one off the plane must clean it."

ANNOUNCEMENT
A flight attendant on a United Air Lines cross-country flight nervously announced about 30 minutes outbound from LA, "I don't know how this happened, but we have 103 passengers aboard and only 40 dinners."

When the passengers' muttering had died down, she continued, "Anyone who is kind enough to give up his or her meal so someone else can eat will receive free drinks for the duration of the flight."

Her next announcement came an hour later. "If anyone wants to change his mind, we still have 29 dinners available!

SAFETY BRIEFING ON CHEAPO AIRLINES
What will they charge for next?
Video.
http://www.youtube.com/watch?v=Q-nX6g148mA

THE SPILL
A plane was taking off from Kennedy Airport (JFK). After it reached a comfortable cruising altitude, the pilot made an announcement over the intercom: "Ladies and gentlemen, this is your captain speaking. Welcome to Flight Number 293, nonstop from New York to Frankfurt. The weather ahead is

good and we should have a smooth and uneventful flight. Now, sit back and relax - OH MY GOD!"

Dead silence followed.

After a few moments, the pilot came back on the intercom and said, "Ladies and Gentlemen, I am so sorry if I scared you earlier. But, while I was speaking, the flight attendant brought me a cup of hot coffee and spilled the coffee all over my lap. You should see the front of my pants!"

A passenger in Coach shouted back, "That's nothing. You should see the back of mine!"

PILOT'S ANNOUNCEMENT
"Ladies and gentlemen, welcome to Glasgow, we hope you enjoyed your flight and thank you for flying Easyjet.
If you didn't enjoy your flight, thank you for flying Ryanair."

PILOT TO PASSENGER
Lady, you want to know if this old airplane is safe to fly?
Just how in the world do you think it got to be this old?
— *Anon*

THE THREE WORST THINGS TO HEAR IN THE COCKPIT:
The second officer says, "Oh s*it!"
The first officer says, "I have an idea"
The captain says, "Hey, watch this!"
— *Anon.*

MURPHY LAWS FOR FREQUENT FLYERS
No flight ever leaves on time unless you are running late and need the delay to make the flight.

If you are running late for a flight, it will depart from the farthest gate within the terminal.

If you arrive very early for a flight, it inevitably will be delayed.

Flights never leave from Gate #1 at any terminal in the world.

If you must work during your flight, you will experience turbulence as soon as you touch pen to paper or turn on your computer.

If you are assigned a middle seat, you can determine who has the seats on the aisle and the window while you are still in the boarding area. Just look for the two largest passengers.

Only passengers seated in window seats ever have to get up to go to the lavatory.
The crying baby on board your flight is always seated next to you.

The best-looking woman/man on your flight is never seated next to you.

The less carry-on luggage space available on an aircraft, the more carry-on luggage passengers will bring aboard.

If you checked two bags, one will arrive early on the conveyor and the other will come last.

STAND UP FLIGHT
Richard Branson's Virgin Blue airline ran ads in newspapers offering the "no chair fare" -- half priced fares for passengers willing to stand for the duration of the flight.
http://bit.ly/dFkCMt

AIRLINE EXPLORES STACKING OF PASSENGERS (Satire)
In its ongoing effort to cut transportation costs and boost profits, United Airlines announced Tuesday that it was exploring the feasibility of herding them into planes and stacking them like cordwood from floor to ceiling.
http://onion.com/hBGEc8

NEGOTIATING AIR FARES
Matt rings up an airline and tries to bargain with him to get the cheapest ticket. Audio.
http://bit.ly/ev4Qts

PHOBIA LIST
Aviophobia or Aviatophobia or Pteromerhanophobia - Fear of flying.

Thaasophobia - Fear of sitting.

Hodophobia - Fear of road travel.

Macrophobia - Fear of long waits.

Glossophobia - Fear of speaking in public.

Agoraphobia - Fear of being in public places like airports.

Laliophobia or Lalophobia - Fear of speaking.

Vaccinophobia - Fear of vaccination.

Xenoglossophobia - Fear of foreign languages.

Xenophobia - Fear of strangers or foreigners.

Consecotaleophobia - Fear of chopsticks.

Phobophobia - Fear of phobias.

JONATHAN WINTERS AS AN AIRLINE PILOT
This long-lost skit features Jonathan Winters at his improvisational best as he's called before an airline commission.
Video.
http://bit.ly/htPJpQ

CAROL BURNETT SHOW- NO FRILLS AIRLINE
Tim is put through the ringer by Carol because he's in the economy section of the airplane while Harvey gets special treatment one seat ahead in First Class.

Video. http://bit.ly/elwASf

AIRLINE PILOT PRACTICAL JOKES
From Monty Python. If I were ever an airline pilot I would be really tempted to try this...
Video. http://bit.ly/f4fPfM

MONTY PYTHON - CHEAP AIRLINE
Video. http://bit.ly/hrb6we

YORKSHIRE AIRLINES
A less-expensive way to fly.
Video. http://bit.ly/hLqH0f

FIRST CLASS vs. ECONOMY
-- Brian Regan, humorist.
Video. http://bit.ly/fKuVea

THOSE SNEAKY LOW COST AIRLINES
SaverJet.com. See what really goes on at the call centre of a low cost airline.
Video. http://bit.ly/f6MTyS

SOUTHWEST AIRLINES FLIGHT ATTENDANT SONG
Southwest Airlines Employee Renee Allen gives the passengers a country hit to take with them.
Video. http://bit.ly/fliVal

Chapter Two
Luggage & Packing

A. Luggage
B. Packing
C. Lost Bags

A. Luggage

FACTOIDS
Some 7,000 bags are lost each day by airlines in the U.S. 97% of the bags are returned to their owners within 24 hours.

San Francisco Airport (SFO) handles some 60,000 bags daily.

Chicago Airport (ORD) processes more than 480 bags per minute.

CHECKING vs. DRAGGING YOUR BAG
Bag-checking fees are one good reason to carry on your bags.

Another is to make it much easier to alter itineraries. For example, If your plane arrives ahead of schedule and you find an earlier connecting flight, you are much more likely to be able to take the earlier flight if the airline does not have to find and move your checked luggage.

Carry-ons also offer the advantage of saving time at check-in and not having to wait for your bag at your destination.

And, most important: carry-ons are less likely to get lost.

"There are two kinds of luggage: Carryon and lost."

If you check your bag, read the airline tag applied to the handle by the counter agent. Confirm that the bag will be directed to your destination. Also confirm that the adhesive has been fully mated because sometimes the tags fall off.

CARRY-ON ALLOWANCES

Now that the airlines have discovered another profit center in checked bags, they are becoming more restrictive about carry-ons and checked bag pricing. Rules may depend on:

Luggage: How large, how heavy, how many bags and other articles.

Your passenger status, and the level/cost of your ticket.

It depends on the airline. For a list of allowances, see your air carrier's website. And
http://bit.ly/agnrd0

SHIPPING YOUR BAGS

You can avoid carrying your bags and the airline checking fees by shipping the luggage via UPS or FedEx. See the Peter Greenberg video.

http://bit.ly/fUdNJr

FLYING WITHOUT LUGGAGE—AROUND THE WORLD

Rolf Potts traveled around the world without a bag. All his needs were in his Scottevest pockets.

http://www.scottevest.com/

He went through 12 countries: U.K. France, Spain, Morocco, Egypt, South Africa, Thailand, Malaysia, Singapore, touched in Australia, went to New Zealand, and came back to the US in 42 days.

http://fxn.ws/grWGBQ

A Peter Greenberg video.
http://www.youtube.com/watch?v=t2z08UtwSjk

LOCKING YOUR LUGGAGE

Many frequent flyers use plastic cinch-ties to lock their suitcases. Using several for each leg of their itinerary, they go through a package of ties rather quickly. Here is a way to "reuse" them.

Get the heavy ties. Do not cinch them up; insert the leading edge into the ratchet receptacle just a few notches. Carry a pair of nail clippers in an outside pocket of the suitcase. On arriving, clip the tie *near* the ratchet receptacle.

When repacking for departure, re-insert the slightly shorter tie.

You should be able to get 8 to 12 uses out of each tie.

Video on TSA locks
http://bit.ly/gguVd8

BALANCE YOUR BAGS FOR EASIER HANDLING

Many people travel with one (9 x 14 x 22"/23 x 40 x 56 cm) wheeled carry-on and one attaché case. The mistake many make is stacking the smaller bag on top of the larger one. This stacking makes (lifting) the load heavier and puts strain on the handle rails.

Slinging the attaché case on the back of the larger bag lowers the center of gravity and balances the load. This arrangement makes the load feel much lighter and much easier to drag.

LUGGAGE WHEELS

Ever have a wheel jam at the beginning of a trip? You will be faced with a choice of carrying the bag or dragging it on a skidding (non-turning) wheel. Not fun.

Protect the wheels. The wheels will not take much bouncing especially when the bag is heavy. Carry your bags up the jetway to the concourse or lift them gently from the plane to the jetway and ease them over the expansion bumps in the floor of the jetway.

When purchasing luggage, favor bags with easily replaceable wheels.

HOW THIEVES OPEN A LOCKED ZIPPERED LUGGAGE BAG
Shocking Video.
http://bit.ly/gioFI3

IDENTIFY YOUR BAGS
Mark your bags with obvious and even obnoxious ribbons; lots of them. Advantages are:

Makes your bags easy to see on the carousel or on carts at smaller, dark airports.

Makes it obvious to others that this is not their bag.
You may not have time to wait until a (embarrassed) fellow-passenger returns to the airport with your luggage.

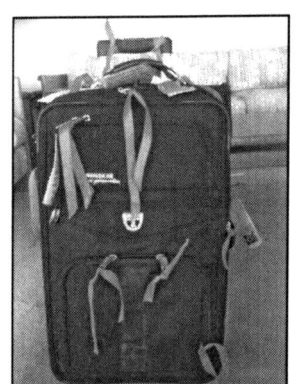

A thief is likely to avoid such an easily identifiable bag. You could spot it, even at a great distance.

Put the ribbons on the drag handle too—so they can be felt by the hand. Do no rely on sight alone. The airport may be dark.

Luggage is often retrieved for passengers by their friends or family. These people are not as familiar with the bags as you are.

Take a photo of your bag with your phone or PDA. Then if a bag is lost or must be located for a flight switch, you can show the photo to the airline agent. They will be relieved and thank you.

Make sure the ribbons are not near the side handle where the airline attaches their routing tag. Because the ribbon might cover a bar code, hiding it from the scanner.

LUGGAGE IDENTIFICATION
Add your flight numbers and name to each checked bag in case the airline bag tag falls off. You can write the information on a piece of white paper tape or use the free baggage tags at the airport.

Print out an extra itinerary an pack it inside your bag.

KEEP ONE HAND ON YOUR BAG
--Terry Brock, USA.

What would you do if you lost your attaché case or purse just before a meeting? What if you lost your computer, video camera, passport and other valuable

items? Discover why you should always keep one hand on your bag.
http://yoursuccess.blogspot.com/
Scroll down to *Bounce Back from a Set Back*

"COAT-SWITCH ROOMS"
Many airlines have a lost-and-found location called the *Coat Switch Room*. If a fellow passenger took your jacket or other garmet from the cabin rack by mistake or if you inadvertently left it behind, it will probably be sent to this special room. The airline will direct people to their Coat-Switch Room.

TAG YOUR CARRY-ON LUGGAGE TOO
Mark the handle of your bag and attaché case with a ribbon or tape. In the rush to deplane, people have been known to grab the wrong bag or case from the overhead compartment.

CARRY-ON BAG TOO THICK FOR THE OVERHEAD BIN?
Some aircraft have narrow overhead bins. Try turning your attaché case around so it goes handle-in/wheels out. Many bags are thinner at the top end. Bins are taller in front than in back.

Some commuter aircraft such as the EMB-120 have slightly taller bins in the back half of the plane. From the outside the bins appear the same but rear bins will accept larger bags.

Also, tape a business card to the bottom of the bag to avoid having your bag picked up by another passenger (in a rush to exit).

LUGGAGE WARRANTIES

Before you purchase suitcases, attaché cases and bags, check the manufacturer's warranties online. The bags of frequent travelers are subjected to a lot of wear and tear. What will the manufacturer cover?

All luggage warranties are not the same. For example:

Samsonite:
"This warranty covers only manufacturing defects and does not cover any damage caused by misuse (such as transportation of unusual items), neglect, accidents, abrasion, exposure to extreme temperatures, solvents, acids, water, normal wear and tear or transport damage (by airlines for example)."
http://bit.ly/fgJSvy

Travel Pro®:
"The Travelpro® warranty covers defects in materials and workmanship but does not cover wear or damage caused by abuse, mishandling, accidental damage, inappropriate selection, or carelessness caused by an airline or other common carrier. In the course of normal handling, your luggage may suffer abrasions, minor cuts, scratches, dents, or soil. Certain component parts such as wheels, bumper feet, leather, etc., will show wear. This wear is not

covered under the warranty. Travelpro® will provide prompt refurbishment services at a nominal cost."
http://www.travelpro.com/warranty.cfm

Briggs & Riley:
"If your Briggs & Riley bag is ever broken or damaged, even if it was caused by an airline, we will repair it free of charge."
http://bit.ly/9YcTj0

To their credit, most of my bags are Travel Pro and have been repaired and replaced several times. Travel Pro stands behind their bags.

Most bags and parts are made in China. The slide fasteners (Zippers) are usually very poor quality. They are easily damaged and injury usually occurs through rough handling by TSA inspectors. Zippers should be run around the corners, all the way to their stops, before lifting the lid of the bag.

TESTING BAGS
Good Housekeeping suggests the best luggage for your travel needs.
Video.
http://bit.ly/fgcsGG

Travel expert Peter Greenberg puts popular luggage brands up to the ultimate test of durability--against a hungry elephant.
http://bit.ly/gm3HGP

PACK AN EXTRA ZIPPERED TOTE/DUFFLE BAG
Then, if your bag is overweight, you can transfer a few (heavier) items to the tote bag. A thin-fabric nylon bag will pack up compactly and take very little room in your luggage.

AIRLINE LIABILITY FOR MISSING LUGGAGE
The Warsaw Convention is an international agreement that regulates liability for international carriage of persons, luggage, or goods.

There is a limit of about $25,000 USD for personal injury and about $26/kg ($57/lb.) of checked luggage. There are limits and many high-value items are not covered. Amounts depend on exchange rates at the time of loss.
http://bit.ly/edVhYZ

B. Packing

BASIC PACKING ADVICE
Savvy travellers know:
Pack only the essentials.
Pack "low-weight, low volume."
Take clothes that won't wrinkle.
Avoid checking bags. Carry them on.

INTERNATIONAL AIR TRAVEL PACKING TIPS
The best way to pack for an international trip is to be aware of airport and airline restrictions for carry-on and check-in luggage. Be adequately prepared for the unexpected. See
http://bit.ly/feurTs

DRAFT A PACKING CHECKLIST
--Dan Poynter, USA.

Pilots use checklists; passengers need checklists. Ever since a prototype B-17 crashed in 1935, aircraft have come with checklists.
http://www.atchistory.org/History/checklst.htm

The next time you pack for a trip, write down each item in your suitcase, attaché case, purse, pockets, etc. On your return, add to the list any items you forgot. Your packing checklist is a growing, evolving document. Keep adding to the list and refining it. A checklist will expedite your packing.

Several years ago, I drove to San Diego the day before a speech. The weather being warm, I drove barefoot with shorts and a tee shirt. Upon arising the next day, I discovered I did not have a belt for my suit. Luckily, I passed a men's store on the way to the speaking venue.

Again several years ago, I flew to a convention in a remote area. Upon arising the next morning, I discovered there was just one set of underwear—the pair I had worn to the venue.

Checklists prevent mistakes.
Pilots use them to avoid accidents.
You should use them to avoid embarrassment.

PUT ADDRESS LABELS ON ALL ITEMS IN YOUR LUGGAGE

Place address labels on all the important items in your luggage. Label your computer, projector, clock, audio equipment, liquid/gels bag, etc.

Provide your full contact information, including your mobile number, so that if the item is found, the finder will be able to notify you with a telephone call or public address announcement.

If you forget your travel clock or needed device at a hotel, you're more likely to get it back if it is labeled with complete contact information.

EFFICIENTLY PACK ITEMS IN ZIPLOC BAGS

Roll your clothing and stow the items in Ziploc bags. Place the bag on the bed or chair and sit on it to expel the air, and then zip it closed. This will save space, make the items of clothing easy to find, keep the clothes clean & dry, and will enable Security personnel to check the contents without opening the bag.

Put all your cables and electrical adapters in a Ziploc bag. This will keep the items together, make them easy to find and will enable Security personnel to check the contents without opening the bag.

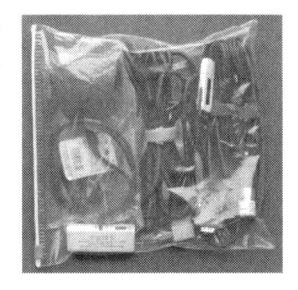

LABEL THAT LIQUIDS/GELS BAG.
Put an address label on that clear plastic bag. Then, if you neglect to retrieve it after clearing the screening area, the Security personnel will know whom to call back to the screening area.

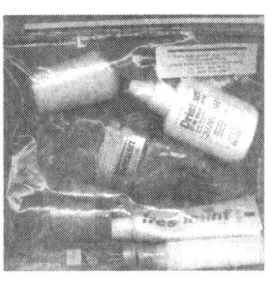

SEPARATING FOREIGN MONEY
Sorting the bills is a challenge; segregating the coins is a nightmare. With coins, the lettering is small and those of several countries have a picture of Queen Elizabeth on one side. It can be hard to tell them apart.

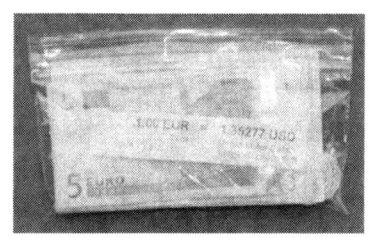

One way to keep the currency segregated is to use snack sized sandwich-type bags. Being transparent, you can see the money on the inside. Being re-sealable, the coins won't fall out.

PRACTICAL TRAVEL GEAR BLOG
Reviews of travel gadgets and travel clothes that are practical and efficient. See
http://practicaltravelgear.com/

GIFTS/GADGETS FOR TRAVELERS
Peter Greenberg shares his favorite gifts for that very special traveler.
Video. http://bit.ly/idiREY
http://bit.ly/hSNP4s

PACK YOUR PAJAMAS—AND WEAR THEM

Last year, Travelodge in the UK experienced more then 400 cases of guests sleepwalking. Ninety-five percent were men in the buff, who appeared at the Reception Desk asking for a newspaper or to check out. Experts blame stress, alcohol abuse, and lack of sleep.
Full article: http://bit.ly/bnpNB7

PROHIBITED ITEMS IN LUGGAGE

Each day in the U.S., passengers place more than 2.2 million prohibited items in their bags. That includes undeclared guns, large knives, and even hand grenades.

In recent months, passengers packed 21 grenades or items that appeared to be grenades in their baggage. In each case, the TSA called in the police to investigate.

In most instances, the grenades were inert and intended to be gifts or novelty items.
http://bit.ly/cGknYK

AIR TRAVEL IN THE U.S. WITH FIREARMS

You may only transport firearms, ammunition and firearm parts in your checked baggage; they are prohibited from carry-on baggage.

Take your locked hard case to check-in. Declare your firearms/ammunition. Be aware of the weight limits per bag.
http://bit.ly/eqWpwx, http://bit.ly/if3Dqi

POLICY CHANGE ALLOWS PASSENGERS TO BRING UNLOADED GUNS ON AMTRAK TRAINS

Guns can be brought aboard trains that have checked baggage service. Gun owners must inform Amtrak officials 24 hours ahead of departure. Unloaded firearms must be packed in hard-sided containers, and will be stored in train lockers.

The change, pushed by gun-rights advocates and ordered by Congress, aligns Amtrak's firearm policy with air travel rules that allow unloaded guns to be stored in locked baggage holds.
http://bit.ly/fNwONe

GOLF CLUBS

If you plan to check a golf bag, consult the airline's website for what you may put in the bag. Most airlines limit you to golf clubs (14 max), golf balls, golf shoes and, maybe, an umbrella. Do not stuff your underwear or other non-golf items in the bag for the trip home.
http://bit.ly/cUEgIY

C. Lost bags

WHAT YOU SHOULD KNOW ABOUT MISHANDLED CHECKED LUGGAGE

Misdirected and lost baggage cost airlines $2.96 billion USD in 2008, about $90 per lost bag-- expenses that are factored into operating costs which are ultimately paid for by passengers. Surprisingly, about 2% of total mishandled bags were actually lost or stolen, an estimated 656,000 bags.
http://bit.ly/df9WPQ

"The scientific theory I like best is that the rings of Saturn are composed entirely of lost airline luggage."
— *Mark Russell, comedian.*

IATA STUDIES MISHANDLED LUGGAGE
Last year, more than 31 million bags--around 1.4% of all checked luggage--arrived late, industry officials say. Roughly 1.8 million bags never arrived. Some take unexplained detours.

To better understand luggage woes, an IATA team conducted weeklong audits of nine major airports, including Dubai, Lisbon and Dallas-Fort Worth. http://on.wsj.com/fssMkP

FILING A CLAIM
What do the airlines owe you for losing your luggage? The bag is not considered "lost" for 21 days. Then the airline will claim "depreciated value."

Make a list of what is inside and keep original purchase receipts. File your claim before you leave the airport. Video. http://bit.ly/fZQaDo

OPEN YOUR CHECKED BAG BEFORE LEAVING THE BAGGAGE AREA
Most luggage loss is from items missing, not the entire bag. If you wait to check your bag's contents until at your destination and then discover an item missing, it is not likely the airline will believe you.
Put expensive and information-sensitive items in your carryon.

UNCLAIMED BAGS GO TO ALABAMA
If the owner cannot be identified and a bag is not claimed, airlines usually send it to the Unclaimed Baggage Center in Scottsboro, Alabama where it is sold. http://www.unclaimedbaggage.com

But if you're thinking UBC might have some item you lost on a recent flight, you are out of luck. UBC cannot help with lost items. By the time luggage reaches UBC, it usually has no form of identification on it and the airlines have already made every effort to reach the rightful owners, including the use of itineraries, personal documents or anything found inside or outside the bags. UBC usually doesn't receive an unclaimed bag for three or four months after the flight.
http://bit.ly/eTP3AJ

See this Peter Greenberg video. http://bit.ly/ep4PVP

WHAT TO DO WHEN SOMETHING IS LOST, MISPLACED OR STOLEN FROM YOUR BAG
Something essential is missing: your mobile-phone charger, computer power supply, camera case, projector remote, etc. Replacing the missing item will be expensive and time consuming and you have to be at a meeting at 9 AM dressed and ready.

Ask the hotel concierge if their Lost & Found has "your missing" item. They have lots of gadgets and accessories. You might even find some useful items you haven't "lost" but could borrow.

Peter Greenberg on the cell-phone charger "lending library." Video. http://bit.ly/fQECYo

BACKUP DOCUMENTATION
Photocopy your itinerary, hotel information, open passport, etc. and place the copies inside your luggage.

Take digital photos of your bags, open passport, itinerary with record locator number, etc. and keep them in your PDA so you can reference them quickly if a bag is lost.

WHAT TO CARRY IN YOUR SMALL PURSE OR POCKETS
Recent aircraft evacuations make us think. Businesspeople have meetings waiting; equipment (aircraft) failures disrupt plans.

In an emergency evacuation, passengers are not supposed to retrieve their luggage. Your carry-on may be consumed in flames or delivered to you several days later. So what can a woman carry in a small purse and a man put in his pockets, especially during takeoffs and landings?

Consider: 24 hours worth of prescription medications, your car keys, passport, mobile phone, local currency and anything else you can't do without for several days. Make this a habit.

Or, wear a "fanny pack."

AIRLINE HELD RESPONSIBLE FOR DELAYED/DAMAGED LUGGAGE

The Air Canada policy sign says "The following damage is considered to be normal wear and [Air Canada] will not accept a claim for: scratches, nicks, missing straps, zipper damage, scuffs, dents, soiling, damage resulting from over packing, damage to wheels, feet, or extending handles."

The Canadian Transport Agency found Air Canada's policy, that it is not responsible for delayed or damaged baggage, violates both international conventions and Canadian law, and must be changed within 90 days.

The ruling will likely affect other airlines as well. Read more: http://bit.ly/d6s2fd

LOST-BAG FORMS

Carry at least one claim form from your regular airline. Take your time and fill it out neatly. Use address labels that canot be misread. This clearly filled form will save time and avoid misinterpretation at the Baggage Claim Office.

Turn in the form even if you are assured the bag will be on the next flight. Keep the copy.

In receipt of your bags, use your mobile phone to photograph any damage. Email the photo to yourself at home for safekeeping.

☺ Humor

LOST LUGGAGE
I couldn't find my luggage at the airport baggage area. So I went to the lost luggage office and told the woman that my bags never showed up.

She smiled and told me not to worry because she was a trained professional and I was in good hands.

Just when I was feeling confident, she asked me, "Has your plane arrived yet?"

CHARGES FOR A SECOND CHECKED BAG.
Some airlines have found ways to charge for other services.
See the humorous video at http://bit.ly/g5VvB5

FLIGHT ANNOUNCEMENT
Flight Attendant (after a delay in taking off):
"I've got some good news and some bad news.
The good news is that the machine that rips the handles off luggage is broken. [cheers, laughter]

The bad news is that our departure will be temporarily delayed while they fix it."

LOST LUGGAGE FUNNY VIDEO
http://bit.ly/cqRxRG

Chapter Three
Health

A. Vaccinations
B. On the Plane
C. On the Ground

This book is not offering health or medical advice. It is suggesting certain ideas a traveler might consider. For details, see the referenced articles and websites, and **consult your health-care professional.**

A. Vaccinations

VACCINE REQUIREMENTS BY COUNTRY
Shots include cholera, hepatitis A, hepatitus B, polio, tetanus, typhoid, yellow fever, diphtheria, Japanese encephaltis, meningococcal meningitis, rabies, tick-borne encephalitis, tuberculosis, etc. Immigration requirements depend on geographical area.

Get specific information on travel documents and health requirements for the area(s) you will be visiting. See http://bit.ly/bVyIO0

FLU SHOTS ARE SEASONAL
--Dan Poynter, USA.

Flu shots become available in the autumn. But autumn seasons are six months apart in the northern and southern hemispheres.

Each year a new flu vaccine is developed to match the different strains of flu virus you are likely to encounter during the winter. In New Zealand, for example, the new vaccine is normally made available in early March, prior to winter there. http://bit.ly/d3O4FT

YELLOW FEVER VACCINATION/REACTION
--Dan Poynter, USA.

You may travel to northern South America or central Africa without a Yellow Fever shot but to return home or go to the next country, you may need a certificate of vaccination issued by the World Health Organization (WHO). See the map at http://bit.ly/avFwcx

See the visa & shot requirements by country. Get specific information on travel documents and health requirements for the area(s) you will be visiting. See http://bit.ly/bVyIO0

If you have a severe adverse reaction to the vaccination and are over 60, your chances of survival are 50%. See paragraph five at http://bit.ly/cSbztB

I spoke in Brasil and then flew on to Johannesburg. Upon entering South Africa, I was asked for my Yellow Fever certificate (shot record) since I had stayed overnight in Brasil. I paid $75 USD for a WHO certified and sealed vaccination and just barely made my air connection to Durban.

After the vaccination, I was light-headed, forgetful, could not concentrate and unable to sleep. Then it got much worse—like a severe case of flu. I blamed my less-than-100% speaking performances on jet lag. Yet crossing multiple time zones had never been a problem in the past.

On my return home I visited my doctor and had blood tests. I was weak and was sleeping 10-12 hours/night. At two presentations, I had to sit down during parts of the speeches.

Full recovery took more than a month.

If you are going to the Amazon Basin or Central Africa, get the Yellow Fever Vaccination before leaving home. Reactions to the vaccination can be life threatening. Do not take the chance that you might react to the shot. See http://bit.ly/hFf9gj

YELLOW FEVER SPECIALISTS
Guide to infectious disease and travel medicine specialists who are licensed to give yellow fever and other travel vaccinations. http://bit.ly/fbUkFP

DIRECTORY OF TRAVEL MEDICINE PROVIDERS
Medical emergencies in distant lands, pre-travel vaccinations, official Yellow Fever vaccine centers, post-travel medical consultation
Click on *Travel Clinic Directory* button at
http://www.istm.org/

B. On the Plane

WHY AIRLINE PASSENGERS GET SICK

When people get sick after traveling, in most cases, it's not because of what they breathed but because of what they touched.

Always assume that the tray table, the button to release the seat back and most surfaces have not been wiped down. The cleaning people spend more time cleaning the lavatory.

WHEN YOU SHOULD BE MOST ALERT IN FLIGHT?

Seventy percent of serious accidents occur during takeoff and landing. Pilot error is a far more likely cause of an airplane crash than mechanical failure or bad weather conditions

Wear your shoes and outer garment until airborne. Sturdy shoes will be more useful in an evacuation. You want shoes to stay on, as you may need protection from hot tarmac or cold snow.

Wear clothing made of natural fibers. Synthetic fabrics could literally melt onto your skin if exposed to the intense heat of an onboard fire.

Keep important papers and medicine on your person in case of emergency evacuation (when you are required to leave all carry-ons behind.)
http://www.Flyana.com/, http://www.joesentme.biz/

DIANA FAIRECHILD SURPRISED THE FLYING WORLD WHEN HER FIRST BOOK, *JET SMART* WAS PUBLISHED IN 1992.

As a former chief international flight attendant who suffered a flight-related deep vein thrombosis and pulmonary embolism, she investigated jet lag and the airline cabin environment, then wrote what passengers need to know about the air, the water, clothing while flying, pesticide sprays, and more.

Since then she has been referred to as an airline passenger activist and a travel guru. Much air-travel health advice on the Internet today is based on her books, the 100+ columns she's written answering questions from passengers, and the nearly 800 media interviews she has given.
http://www.Flyana.com/tv.html

AIR TRAVEL MORE THAN DOUBLES BLOOD CLOT RISK

Deep-Vein Thrombosis
Long-distance travel can lead to potentially fatal blood clots in some people--and the risk grows with the length of the trip.

Deep vein thrombosis, or DVT, is a medical condition where a blood clot forms in a deep vein, usually in the leg, calf, or pelvis. It occurs when long-term pressure constricts a vein, making it easier for a clot to form. It is more likely to occur during a flight. With reduced air pressure, the veins swell. With dry air, the blood thickens. Most planes are pressurized to 8,000-feet/2438 m.

If such a clot dislodges and travels to the lungs, it can cause a potentially fatal condition called "pulmonary embolism."

Symptoms of DVT may take several days to occur.

Some of the things you can do to avoid DVT is to sit properly, drink lots of water, and get up to walk around the cabin. If you are susceptible to DVT, you might even wear compression stockings and take aspirin to thin the blood. Ask your doctor for more information.
http://bit.ly/dmZEkv
http://bit.ly/aOEpla
http://bit.ly/hp0kdV
http://www.Flyana.com/
http://bit.ly/av1mZt

EXERCISING WHILE YOU TRAVEL
Commutercise is a workout plan that can be done while sitting. See
http://www.Commutercise.com
http://www.Flyana.com/

SLEEPING ON PLANES
Pills, eyeshades, earplugs, and noise-canceling headsets.

If you can sleep during transit you may feel better on arrival and the trip may seem shorter. For many frequent flyers the best part of airline travel is sleeping. Here are some slumber aids other than sleeping pills. See
http://www.Flyana.com/

http://www.nojetlag.com/jetlag_news.html
http://bit.ly/c6v8ou

Some travelers report good results from nonprescription Melatonin. Others like Valerian (600 mg. Nature's Plus #7354). Some use both.

For details on usage, etc., see
http://en.wikipedia.org/wiki/Melatonin,
http://en.wikipedia.org/wiki/Valerian_(herb)
and other web sites. Consult your health professional.

Aromatherapy
Some passengers like lavender oil for aiding sleep. They put a few drops on a pillow or garment. Lavender may also help you sleep in an unfamiliar (hotel) bed.

Eyeshades block daylight and make a great difference for some people.

Earplugs will dampen the drone of the engines and can be helpful to people who are not accustom to background noises.

Noise-canceling headsets
The best known are made by Bose® and may fit *on the ears* or *surrounding the ears*.

Sony® makes a much more compact set of noise canceling *earplugs*. They may be plugged into your music player or used without the audio. They're powered by a single AAA battery.

For most ears, the 'in-the-ear types' are best because they seal against the ear canal and block the drone of the engines.

WHY AIR ON PLANES SEEMS STAGNANT
Because it is.

Most airliners are pressurized to 8,000-feet/2438 m. With reduced pressure, there is less oxygen available, night vision may become slightly impaired, and fatigue levels may rise. It is normal to feel tired after a long flight.

The cockpit gets the most new air, followed by First Class, Business Class, and Economy. And, in Economy, there are more people packed into the cabin—sharing the available oxygen.

Aircraft air circulates across seat rows, not down the length of the plane.

Modern airliners use HEPA filters to reduce the spread of airborne pathogens in recirculated air.
http://bit.ly/d9K0FR,
http://en.wikipedia.org/wiki/HEPA

DISINFECTANT AND INSECTICIDE SPRAYS ON PLANES
What, why and how to avoid it.

The World Health Organization approves the spraying of insecticides in aircraft cabins in order to try to prevent crop-ruining insects from immigrating between countries. The procedure is called "disinsection" i.e. killing insects, and it is done in both "occupied" and "unoccupied" airplane cabins.

The most vulnerable passengers are those who are sensitive or have compromised immune systems, as well as the elderly, and infants.

Spraying may be done any time: after departure, before landing, or after landing.

You can wear a mask and launder your clothes after the flight. Don't bother asking for the plane's oxygen bottle. Its mask has holes to equalize air pressure.

For a list of countries that require spraying, see
http://www.flyana.com/pest.html
http://www.allergyuk.org/art_aircraft.aspx

JET LAG
Giving a 100% performance in a distant venue
--Dan Poynter, USA.

Whether you are negotiating a business deal or delivering a speech, you want to be sharp and clear headed. Imagine your frustration and embarrassment if your speaking is slower than usual, slurring your words and/or forgetting where you are in your presentation.

Businesspeople face many challenges with venue, audiences, meeting planners, transportation, and so on. Crossing multiple time zones causes one major challenge. Most road warriors are not affected to a great degree by a two- or three-hour time change such as traveling across the U.S. But longer international travel is another matter.

Diana Fairechild (flyana.com) says jet lag (desynchronosis) can cause insomnia, daytime sleepiness, poor concentration, irrational/unreasonable thinking, lack of energy/motivation, swelling of the limbs, disorientation, and slower reaction times. In other words, your body is out of whack.

When you are suffering from jet lag, your mental and physical reflexes are slower. Businesspeople want successful negotiations. Professional speakers want every presentation to be a 100% performance. They want to do their best and audiences deserve to get what they are paying for. Any performance less than 100% is unacceptable for the true professional.

In 1976, I was Chief of Delegation for the U.S. Parachute Team. We flew from California to Warrendorf in Northern Germany (9 time zones) and went into World-Championship competition the next day. The first round was a disaster for the U.S. team; the eight-person team was sluggish and disoriented as they performed their aerial maneuvers.

Skydiving teams complete a formation and then transition to several more configurations while plummeting at 120 mph. The aerial maneuvers are evaluated and timed by judges with high-powered video devices. The competitors blamed their poor performance on unexpected aircraft configuration;

the door was on the opposite side from what they were used to. The next jump was not much better. The Championships dragged on for more than a week due to poor weather. The U.S. Team performed a little better each day, squeaking into Gold Medals on the tenth and final round of competition.

The 1977 World Meet was in Gatton, Queensland, Australia (7 time zones. More miles but fewer time zones). I had read that NASA estimates it takes about one day to regain normal rhythm and energy levels for each time zone crossed. I persuaded the Board of Directors to send the team to Australia three weeks prior to the Championships so they could train on site. It cost more to train outside the U.S. but training at home would amount to false economy.

On arrival, we went to the drop zone (parachute center) and, of course, the team members wanted to make a training jump. We explained the jet lag challenge and told them they were to be "grounded tourists" for at least a week. Jumps were expensive; wasted jumps would be a foolish expenditure. They begged, they sniveled and they cajoled. Finally the Team Leader gave in and up they went. Their choreographed maneuvers were sluggish and incomplete; they performed terribly! A wiser skydiving team spent the next week recovering from jet lag on the beach.

Some companies have a formal policy of "no business meetings the first day after a flight" but this guideline fails to recognize that jet lag can last a week or more.

A professional athlete's performance is measured at every competitive attempt. Businesspeople are like athletes to the extent that they must perform at 100% of their abilities. An 85% or 90% performance is not a winner.

There are two issues in jet lag.
A. The affect of travel across time zones on your performance.
    1. Resetting your body's clock to local time.
B. The affects on the body of traveling in a plane.

A. Time zones.
The issue is time zones; upsetting your body's clock, not distance. While north-south travelers may suffer from air travel, these journeys do not disturb circadian rhythms; your body is still operating on the same eat-sleep schedule. Bodily distress in east-west travel is due also to the zones.

On the other hand, according to Diana Fairechild, author of *Jet Smarter: The Air Traveler's Rx*, "Flying over the Equator can reduce our ability to function in many ways such as coordination (physical), clear thinking (mental), and gut feeling (emotional)."
Many people report that flying east is harder on them than going west. Flying from North America to the UK is likely to be a greater jet lag challenge than flying the other way to Australia.

"Jet lag is not psychological, it is cycle-logical."
--Diana Fairechild.

What you can do. If you have booked an exotic distant venue and plan to extend your stay for a holiday, vacation first and work toward the end of your stay. Let your body catch up as much as possible. You will also have an opportunity to get to know the country and pick up some informational items to work into your small talk, business presentation, or speech. If you must work soon after your arrival, try to schedule it during your at-home awake time. Are you a morning person or night owl?

See the Jet Lag Calculator
http://www.bodyclock.com/
To calculate out how many time zones you will cross, see
http://www.timeanddate.com/worldclock/

Adjusting to local time. The body is accustomed to a regular rhythm of day and night. Light and dark affect your biological functions (circadian rhythms), including when you eat and sleep. Those with a fixed daily routine suffer more when their routine is upset.

What you can do. Sleep before you leave; begin your travels well rested, so that you have an extra supply of energy to draw upon. Research shows the more tired you are when you travel, the more you will struggle with jet lag. Trying to catch up on sleep *while* you are traveling does not always work. Even a fully reclining island seat in First Class is not a substitute for your own bed.

For long flights, try to schedule takeoff near your usual bedtime. You will have a better chance of a (nearly) full night's sleep.

Do not eat before sleeping just because they are serving food. Eat only if it is at your normal mealtime. Digestion expends your body's energy and may inhibit your ability to sleep.

When you arrive, adopt local time. Sunlight will go to work resetting your body's clock. Get outside in the bright sunlight (without sunglasses) whenever possible. If you are not getting enough sleep at night, take a *very short* nap during the day.

Sleeping pills may induce sleep but they have no effect on re-aligning the body's biological imbalance caused by traveling to a different time zone.

Melatonin may help decrease jet lag. It is a hormone sold in supplement form at health food stores. Try taking 1-3 milligrams of melatonin at bedtime for several days *after* you arrive at your destination. Read the directions.

B. Staying healthy in a plane.

Sleeping on the plane may be tougher for people on their first trip abroad because they are too excited to sleep.

What you can do.

Environment. Use earplugs and eyeshades to shut out some of the noise and light.

Hydration. Sip water throughout the flight (8 oz/.24 liters) per hour. Dry membranes are more susceptible to infection.

Diet. Generally, proteins keep you awake and carbs make you sleepy.

Exercise. See the seat-exercise instructions in the in-flight magazine. Walk around the cabin of the plane to exercise your limbs and stretch your muscles.

Of course, the usual warnings about smoking, overeating, alcohol and caffeine apply.

Some people swear by *No Jet Lag* pills, a homeopathic, available in many health food and travel stores. See http://www.NoJetLag.com.

Sports people compete against each other to improve their performances. Businesspeople compete with themselves to become the best they can be. Jet lag affects both and is a challenge that can be confronted and minimized.

A lot of detailed jet lag advice is available on the web. For example, see
http://www.flyana.com.
http://bit.ly/f9Q5Hu
http://www.StopJetLag.com/stopjetl.html

REDUCING JET LAG WHEN TRAVELING ABROAD
Video.
http://bit.ly/i91RWo

PINE BARK EXTRACT MAY ALLEVIATE JET LAG
A new study published in the journal of Minerva Cardioangiologica (publishes papers on heart and vascular diseases) reveals Pycnogenol, pine bark extract from the French maritime pine tree, reduces jetlag in passengers by nearly 50 percent.
http://www.physorg.com/news145108851.html
http://bit.ly/cYTBcM

A BLUE PILL FOR JET LAG?
-–Joe Sherren, Canada.

Viagra, amongst other things, does change sleep function, and it may facilitate the recovery from jet lag
http://bit.ly/auHeRC

RADIATION
Increased air travel may be responsible for a jump in the amount of naturally occurring radiation to which flyers are exposed.

Airline pilots have more chance of developing one form of leukemia.

This is blamed on "cosmic radiation" from the sun, which is more intense at the altitudes reached by modern aircraft.

However, the increased risk of acute myeloid leukemia was noticed only in pilots who had logged more than 5,000 flying hours in their careers. Experts have stressed that even frequent flyers will rarely accumulate a high dose.
http://news.bbc.co.uk/2/hi/health/557340.stm
http://bit.ly/cswl4e

One study shows that vitamin B_3, niacin, minimizes radiation damage.
http://bit.ly/guhOSd

FLYING AFTER SCUBA DIVING

The question is often asked, "Why do I have to wait to fly after diving?" The answer to the question is simply "pressure." Consider sea level as the baseline and at this level we all have one atmosphere of weight on us (without us even noticing it!). For every 33 feet/10m of seawater we descend, add another atmosphere to the pressure. This pressure causes nitrogen to go into solution in our blood and our plasma becomes supersaturated.

The opposite is true for ascending to altitude with a decrease in pressure. It is the reduction in pressure that causes nitrogen to come out of solution and to bubble (like opening a bottle of carbonated CO_2 beverage which is under pressure).

A minimum surface interval of 12 hours is recommended before ascent in a commercial aircraft [8000 foot (2438 m.) cabin]. Allow 24 hours if your dive more than 33'/10m in depth.

See the chart and explanation:
http://scuba-doc.com/flyngaft.htm

SWELLING DURING FLIGHT
Many passengers notice that their feet swell during flight.

Wear loose shoes and clothing. Shoes half a size larger may be more comfortable. If you have a plaster cast, have it split by a health-care professional before the flight. Allow for expansion.

FLYING AFTER DONATING BLOOD
Blood donors should wait 24 hours before flying.
http://www.leftseat.com/blood.htm

DON'T DRINK THE "PLANE" WATER
--Dan Poynter, USA.
Water served on airliners is not filtered and rarely tested. When independently tested, all kinds of bacteria are found.

Diana Fairechild, a former international chief flight attendant, reports seeing a plane's water tank being refilled in Mumbai, India, with a garden hose.

Drink only bottled water on planes, at least 8 oz. (.24 liters) per hour, and do not consume coffee or tea unless you confirm they are not made with "plane water."

Flight attendants have been known to refill the plastic bottles with plane water. They sometimes refer to it as "Tappian."

Heating water to make the beverages is not likely to kill the bacteria. The water is heated only briefly and then only to the pressure altitude of 8,000-feet/2438 m. At that altitude the boiling temperature of water is much lower.

Some frequent flyers request carbonated water without ice to make sure of the water's origin but carbonated water ("mit gas" in German) may cause bloating. Same for other carbonated beverages.

See
http://www.news-medical.net/?id=7407
http://bit.ly/hE79Zm
http://bit.ly/gnIdQI
http://www.greenhome.com/info/news/77.shtml
http://bit.ly/htkODB

United video about coffee on the plane. Humor.
http://www.youtube.com/watch?v=b43NMIBffiU

WOULD YOU LIKE A SLICE OF LIME IN YOUR WATER?
--Larry Ohlhauser, MD, Edmonton, Canada.

No thank you!
"Even in advanced countries, many slices of lemon and lime contain E. Coli bacteria."

PAYING FOR FOOD AND DRINK
If you want meals and/beverages on flights in the US, carry both cash and a credit card. Some airlines require cash only and some will only accept plastic.

Pull out a US bill and you will notice the statement "This note is legal tender for all debts public and private."

It would appear that while above the United States, airlines have to accept U.S. cash by law.

JOINING THE MILE-HIGH CLUB
Sex at high altitude.

Few are able to join, and the barriers are formidable. Once you find a willing partner, you need to navigate your way through a plane that is pretty crowded and hope a line doesn't form outside the door. Next, you have to cope with the cramped conditions in the plane's lavatory. For suggestions on how to join the club, see
http://read.bi/cNgtAN

FLYING WHILE PREGNANT
While most women heed airline rules against flying during the last four or five weeks of pregnancy or comply with requirements about providing a medical certificate from a doctor, some manage to conceal their condition or lie about how far along they are so they can fly to where they plan to go.

Since 2007, babies have been born aboard planes flying from Chicago to Salt Lake City; on a domestic flight in Malaysia; and on long-haul flights from the Netherlands to Boston, from Hong Kong to Australia, and from Germany to Atlanta.

The rules now are based on honesty and (the idea) that a pregnant mom is going to protect her unborn.

Travel through the first trimester of pregnancy is more risky than other trimesters.

Air travel during the second trimester is the safest.
Air travel during the third trimester is a challenge that increases as your due date approaches.
http://bit.ly/9gY7k7
http://bit.ly/9zwJD1
http://bit.ly/bnVZ8p

TRAVELING WITH A DISABILITY
Some 49-million people in the U.S. are disabled to some degree.
An estimated 17-million disabled passengers fly in the U.S. each year.

The Society for Accessible Travel & Hospitality (SATH), founded in 1976, is an educational nonprofit membership organization whose mission is to raise awareness of the needs of all travelers with disabilities, remove physical and attitudinal barriers to free access and expand travel opportunities in the United States and abroad. Members include travel professionals, consumers with disabilities and other individuals and corporations who support SATH's mission.
http://www.sath.org/

Also see
http://bit.ly/9iRm4w
http://bit.ly/b4tmKt
http://bit.ly/ffgjjF
http://bit.ly/a4Dv5R

WHEELCHAIR SLOW IN COMING?
The wheelchair service is usually subcontracted by the airport's city. Only rarely is it provided by your airline. Quick wheelchair service may not be a top priority for cities.

C. On the Ground

PREPARING IN CASE YOU GET SICK AWAY FROM HOME
Only about 40 percent of American companies have any type of travel risk-management program in place to help employees deal with medical emergencies, kidnapping and extortion threats or any of the other problems that can occur when traveling abroad.

Read what you can do about this challenge.
http://nyti.ms/dAIkYj

STAYING HEALTHY WHILE TRAVELLING
Preparing for the trip, vaccinations, what to carry in a first aid kit and health-travel tips. See
http://bit.ly/9ErOba

AIRPLANE EXHAUST
The fumes from airplanes are to blame for more annual deaths than actual airplane crashes.

Around 10,000 deaths per year can be blamed on airplane pollution. Compare that to 1,000 annual deaths caused by crashes.

The most common deadly conditions linked to pollution are cardiovascular disease and respiratory ailments like lung cancer.

Most of the deaths are caused by emissions at cruising altitudes over 3,000 feet--not takeoff and landing, whose emissions are monitored and controlled.

On the other hand, emissions from ships kill some 60,000 people each year. Then we have automobiles.
http://aol.it/aE1GcT

WHERE TO *GO*
Finding a clean **restroom** while traveling can be a challenge. This site has reviews and maps of toilet locations worldwide that you can print out and carry with you!
http://www.thebathroomdiaries.com/
Australia specific: http://www.toiletmap.gov.au/

SOME OTHER USES FOR TOOTHPASTE
--Lori Allen, USA.

When I was young, my mom would take water rings off our coffee table with toothpaste. Today, I use toothpaste for a number of things... especially when I'm traveling and have to limit the amount of "stuff" I bring with me.

1. Bee sting ointment. If you can't get ice for your bee sting, dab a little toothpaste on it. It's rumored to be the very best home remedy. (Also works to relieve the itch of a mosquito bite.)

2. An overnight pimple cream. I find that if I dab just a spot of toothpaste on a rebellious pimple before I go to bed, it's nearly gone by morning.

3. Jewelry cleaner. Simply put a small amount of toothpaste on a soft cloth and rub it on your dry jewelry. Use a soft cotton swab for the smaller, hard-to-reach spots. Then rinse it off.

4. Shoe cleaner. Toothpaste and a cloth, or old toothbrush, are great for cleaning the white rubber parts of tennis shoes.

--Lori Allen is the director of AWAI's Travel Division.
You'll find more tips like these at
http://www.thetravelwriterslife.com/travel_tips/

MORE HEALTH WEBSITES

Helios Homoeopathy, http://www.helios.co.uk/

International Society of Travel Medicine (ISTM). http://www.istm.org/

MASTA. Find your nearest travel clinic.
http://www.masta-travel-health.com/

Chapter Four
Security & Safety

A. Security in the Airport
B. Security on the Plane
C. Safety off the Airport

A. Security in the Airport

SPEEDING YOUR WAY THROUGH SECURITY
Put your watch, pen, phone, and other metal objects in your purse, attaché case, or a separate Zip Lock bag.

Men: wear a belt with a plastic buckle.
Don't spend time undressing at the checkpoint.
For non-metallic belts, see Magellan's and REI.
http://bit.ly/cuqXFK or http://bit.ly/aolEG8

Peter Greenberg video on speeding your way through the airport and Security.
http://bit.ly/hjxHax, http://bit.ly/eq2XMj

FLY THROUGH AIRPORT SECURITY
Video with Jonathon E. Stewart
http://bit.ly/aDm0JY

LIGHTERS IN U.S. CARRY-ONS
--Susan Foster, USA.

TSA is no longer banning common lighters in carry-on luggage.

Torch lighters remain banned in unchecked bags.

In 2006, 11,616,217 lighters were confiscated by the TSA. (that's 22,000 per day!).

PRIORITY SCREENING LINES
Which airports have shorter lines for frequent flyers? Here is a partial list.

1K: United Mileage Plus Premier Executive 1K status. Awarded to members who fly 100,000 actual miles or 100 paid segments in a calendar year.

1P: United Mileage Plus Premier Executive status. Awarded to members who fly 50,000 miles or 60 segments in a single calendar year.

2P: United Mileage Plus Premier status. Awarded to members who fly 25,000 actual miles or 30 paid segments.

Atlanta - 1P/F/C, "Airline Club Members"
Charlotte, NC - @ checkpoint B for US Airways Preferred Members
Chicago - 2P
Denver - 2P, but experience says 1P
Dulles [IAD] - 2P
Honolulu - 2P
Las Vegas - 1K
London Heathrow Terminal 3 - C/F Only
Los Angeles - 2P
Minneapolis - 2P
Orange County/John Wayne - 2P
New York [JFK] - 2P
Philadelphia - Access thru Terminal C
Phoenix - 2P
Pittsburgh, PA - F/all elites

Portland, Oregon - 2P
Providence, Rhode Island - All elites, use WN Business Select
San Diego - 1P/*G
San Francisco - Domestic is 3P+, International is GS and F only
San Jose - combined elite security line for all airlines
Seattle - 1P
Washington Dulles [IAD] - 2P
Washington National [DCA] -2P
http://bit.ly/fhV5LZ

BOARDING PASSES, from paper to PDA

No need to visit the hotel business center to print out paper boarding passes. Now you can download the boarding pass to your PDA or smart phone.

See the explanatory video at
http://bit.ly/a9i9gE

STAR ALLIANCE AUTO DOC CHECK

Singapore Airlines was the first carrier to check visas/documentation automatically.
http://bit.ly/ek0vVu

OK TO CARRY KNIVES ON PLANES IN INDIA

The Bureau of Aviation Security, Government of India, Bulletin 34/2002 limits kirpan knife lengths to 22.86 cms (9 inches) and the length of the blade to 15.24 cms (6 inches). See
http://www.sgpc.net/news/kirpan.asp

U.S. D.O.T. INVOKES NEW LOOSE-STOWAGE LITHIUM BATTERY RULE

In response to the theory that Li-ion batteries are a potential fire hazard, The Department of Transportation has adopted a rule.

Lithium batteries must in installed in their devices (mobile phones, cameras, computers, etc.) Spare (extra or "extended") batteries must be in individual plastic bags. Do not permit a loose battery to come in contact with metal objects, such as coins, keys, or jewelry; shorting across the electrical contacts could occur. The D.O.T. said that loose lithium batteries could short-circuit and create a fire hazard in cargo holds.

For "spare" lithium batteries, the carryon-bag limit is two. The checked bag limit is zero.

This restriction applies primarily to professional and industrial-use batteries and does not affect most lithium batteries used in consumer electronics like laptops and mobile phones.

Check the back of your batteries for the type. Look for "Li-ion."
For the DOT Rule, see
http://bit.ly/eksM5D

MOBILE PHONES AND AIRPORT SECURITY
--Joe Sherren, Canada.

If you are asked to test your cell phone at the airport, this is the reason: Cell phone guns have arrived. The video clip shows how cell phone guns operate. These phones are not in North America yet but they are in use overseas.

Beneath the digital phone face is a .22 calibre handgun capable of firing four rounds in rapid succession using the standard telephone keypad.

European law enforcement officials are stunned by the discovery of these deadly decoys. They say phone guns are changing the rules of engagement in Europe. Only when you have one in your hand do you realize that they are heavier than a regular cell phone.

Be patient if Security asks to look at your cell phone or to turn it on to show that it works. They have a good reason! See http://bit.ly/gqvHJr

HOW MANY EYES ARE WATCHING YOU IN AIRPORT SECURITY?

The Behavior Detection Officer (BDO) program utilizes non-intrusive behavior observation and analysis techniques to identify potentially high-risk passengers. BDOs are trained to detect individuals exhibiting behaviors that indicate they may be a threat to aviation and/or transportation security. The program is a derivative of other successful behavioral analysis programs that have been employed by law enforcement and security personnel both in the U.S. and around the world.

TSA's BDO-trained security officers are screening travelers for involuntary physical and physiological reactions that people exhibit in response to a fear of being discovered.

Learn about Behavior Detection Officers.
http://bit.ly/gtNGPH

WHERE IS YOUR DATA?
Last year in the UK, 9,000 USB sticks were left in clothes taken to local dry cleaners. One dry cleaner in London said he is getting an average of 1 USB stick every 2 weeks, another said he had found at least 80 in the past year.

6,193 handheld devices such as laptops, iPods, and memory sticks are forgotten at the back of taxis every 6 months! Questions arise about security.
http://bit.ly/aEQ6og

U.S. TSA REQUIRES REGISTRATION BEFORE FLYING
As part of the Transportation Security Administration's Secure Flight program, American and United airlines are requiring passengers to provide more personal information when they book flights.

Passengers must provide their full name, including middle name or middle initial, gender, date of birth and a redress case number if that person was previously put on the No-Fly or Watch list by mistake.

The name provided must match the name as written on a valid government-issued ID that the passenger will present at the airport. Be careful when you enter your personal information into your online flight record. If you make an error, it may be difficult to get corrected.

For more information on the Secure Flight Program, visit the TSA website at
http://bit.ly/fRYTID, http://bit.ly/bnrBs3
http://bit.ly/dwWdDB

AIRPORTS MAY USE AN ALTERNATIVE TO TSA
In the original Homeland Security agreement, airports can opt out of using the TSA if they hire on legitimate private security to perform the tasks the TSA was created for.
http://exm.nr/h10KHQ, http://bit.ly/gFJHuB

WHAT HAPPENS TO THE ITEMS SURRENDERED TO AIRPORT SECURITY.
In 2006 alone, screeners took in more than 13 million items in the U.S. Read about the craziest items and find out where you can buy them. See http://bit.ly/bRuR1z

TSA: FINDERS-KEEPERS
If you empty your pockets of change, and fail to retrieve it, when going through airport Security in the U.S., the Transportation Security Administration will keep it. Abandoned change used to go to the General Fund of the U.S. Treasury. Nearly $90,000 USD has been collected in the past three years at LAX, alone.

WHO GETS SCREENED?
Passengers and flight crews. The crew has to endure the same screening as the passengers. On the other hand, the baggage loaders, cleaners, caterers, and refuelers are only subjected to occasional random screening.

TSA HAS AN IPHONE APP
An iPhone app from the Transportation Security Administration offers guidance on prohibited items, security wait times, and packing tips.

Titled *My TSA*, the free app lets you fill in the blank to ask if you can bring various objects through the airport Security checkpoint. See the App Store.

BRIEF CHILDREN ON SECURITY
Your children must undergo the exact same screening process as everyone else.

Explain the air travel rules to your child or children. Depending on their age, this can be a fairly difficult task. Tell each child he or she will have to enter the scanner. Children who can walk are encouraged to go through it alone. Your child may be pulled aside for a pat-down just like everyone else.
http://bit.ly/aMNvVv

LOST GIRL FINDS KINDNESS AT O'HARE
A stranded traveler offers a chance to share some old generosity.
http://bit.ly/aNlc5v

WATCH FOR THIEVES IN AIRPORT SECURITY

Put your luggage and binned items on the belt and make sure they are going into the machine before you approach the body-scan arch. If someone ahead of you sets off the body-scan alarm, go in front of him or her while they take of the offending belt or other article. Don't ask; be assertive—move.

Do not talk to colleagues in Security; watch your personal items on the other side of the scanner.

One common scenario is for one thief to pass quickly though the scanner. The second is positioned in front of you and wears metal to set off the alarm. Attention is draw to the second thief who is fumbling around looking for the offending metal. Meanwhile, the first thief picks up your computer or bag and blends into the crowd.

SAFEGUARDING YOUR COMPUTER AT THE AIPORT

Nearly 12,000 laptops are lost in airports in the United States each week. Yes, 12,000!

Only one-third of travelers recover the lost devices.

Between 65 and 70 percent of the lost laptops are never reclaimed. Many laptops are lost at security checkpoints

53 percent of business travelers surveyed carry sensitive corporate information on their laptop. 65 percent of those who carry confidential information have not taken steps to protect it while traveling. 42 percent of respondents say they do not back up their data.

A major challenge at TSA Security checkpoints is that many laptops look alike. It is too easy for a nearby passenger to pick up the wrong computer and place it in his or her bag. They will not notice the mistake until after they reach their destination.

Reduce this "computer swap" tendency by placing a unique and noticeable sticker or business card on the top of your notebook computer. Other passengers will quickly recognize the computer does not belong to them.

Many laptops are picked up by thieves while going through Security and in other areas of the airport such as restaurants.

Read the article. http://bit.ly/9MFvT1

See the story on the statistics by Dell Computers at http://dell.to/9Zah4d

Download the complete study at http://dell.to/94OvzM

LABEL YOUR LAPTOP

A label on top notifies other passengers going through Security that the computer does not belong to them.

A label on the underside is for the benefit of the Security officers.

Provide your full contact information, including your *mobile* number, so that if the device is found, airport personnel will be able to notify you with a public address announcement or call.

EXPERIENCES IN AIRPORT SECURITY--DUBAI
--Roger Harrop, roger@rogerharrop.com, UK.

"I, like most professional speakers, am "joined at the hip" to my speakers bag--which never leaves my sight. With the usual contents of projector, speakers, laptop, remote, flash drive, clock, etc., it inevitably gets looked at by the X-ray guys--without any problem.

But here's a new twist--on leaving (but not on arriving!) Dubai airport I was told that extension leads (power cords or extension cords in the U.S.) were not allowed and I had to surrender it.

EXPERIENCES IN AIRPORT SECURITY--FRANKFURT
---Dan Poynter, http://ParaPublishing.com, USA.

I carry two computers; one is a PowerPoint backup for the other. In going through Security at the

Frankfurt Airport, the security guard looked into the bin and said: "ach, 2 computer--ist verboten."

My stomach churned. I looked up to see him smiling. Who says Germans don't have a sense of humor?

EXPERIENCES IN AIRPORT SECURITY—TEL AVIV
-- Randall Munson, http://www.CreativelySpeaking.com, USA

It was my most recent departure from Tel Aviv, Israel. As usual, I was carrying magic props that I use in my keynote presentations. One of them was a "boo-boo-bar" made from a 6" metal pipe that, naturally, caught the attention of the airport Security Agent.

I explained that I'm a magician and showed the Security Agent the trick to assure him it wasn't a pipe bomb. Then he pointed at another prop and asked what that was so I demonstrated another magic effect.

That went on and on. At first I thought he was being very careful but then I came to realize he was actually enjoying a free magic show. I didn't want to appear to be uncooperative but after the 5th or 6th trick I mentioned my flight time and he immediately passed me through Security.

I almost missed my plane but, hey, I gained a new fan. I guess it shows that even the world's top security people are still people.

EXPERIENCES IN AIRPORT SECURITY
--Michael A. Podolinsky, Singapore.

I ALMOST lost my Targus computer lock cable but they listened to my argument, saw my blond hair, and figured I was not one of the 'bad guys.' I think they reasoned the cable could be used it as a garrote. Remember the Godfather movie? The wire goes around the neck, pull tight... silent and deadly. Power cords could do the same thing.

But hey... they allow belts, (same as power cords), CDs (crack one down the middle and have two 'knives') and 100 other things a pro could use.

What shocked me was when they used to NOT allow fingernail clippers. "I've got nail clippers... give me your plane or I'll trim you to death!"

AIRPORT SECURITY--FRANKFURT
-- Jeff Abelman, USA.

I was returning from the German Speakers Association convention. After my carry-on bag passed through the scanner, this tall, very stern looking Security man stepped up to my bag and pulled it aside and motioned for me to follow him to the end of the line--and two more very big stern-looking as well German Guards stepped behind him and myself.

He asked if this was my bag to which I replied yes, thinking, OK what is he seeing that is going to make me possibly miss my flight. He then says "I've noticed with the scanner that you have an authentic German Beer Stein in your bag. Is it yours?"

"Yes it's a souvenir" I replied.

He then goes on to say that there have been problems with Americans taking German Beer Steins home to America and that he needs to be assured that I won't cause any problems and if I make an affidavit then he can allow me to take it out of the country.

Thinking it would get me out of there I said "no problem, what do I do?" He says "Raise your right hand and repeat after me, I promise to not insult German Bier history by putting cheap American beer like Miller Lite or Budweiser in the mug for as long as I own it." So I repeated his words and we had a good laugh, and greatly relieved, off I went.

Who says the Germans have no sense of humor.

EXPERIENCES IN AIRPORT SECURITY--OTTAWA

I was at the Ottawa, Canada, airport, checking in when an airport employee asked, 'Has anyone put anything in your baggage without your knowledge?'

To which I replied, 'If it was without my knowledge, how would I know?'

He smiled knowingly and nodded, 'That's why we ask.'

CUSTOMS: DOGS CAN DETECT MORE THAN DRUGS
--Dan Poynter, USA.

And they can sense traces after prohibited items have been removed from the luggage.

On a recent trip to Auckland, I was waiting at the conveyor for my suitcase when I was approached by an officer with a drug-sniffing dog. The canine became excited upon encountering my wheeled attaché case.

The officer asked if I had any fruit or vegetables in my case. I replied that there were two bananas and an apple in the case between Los Angeles and Sydney. But that they had been consumed hours ago. He asked to see the bag and search it.

Australia, New Zealand, and many other countries not only prohibit the import of drugs, they do not want fresh vegetables or fruit brought into their countries.

Even if you remove the offending items, the odor lingers on.

EXPERIENCES IN AIRPORT SECURITY—NITRATES
--Dan Poynter, USA.

Going through Security in Portland, Oregon, my suitcase was pulled aside for secondary screening. The TSA officer was probably alarmed by seeing computer/projector cables and spare batteries on the X-ray screen. Another officer swabbed the bag, including the handle. He checked the circular piece of cloth in a detection machine. Alarmed, he swabbed and checked a second time. Then a third.

The officer asked if I had been on a farm (nitrates are in fertilizer) or had handled firearms (nitrates are in explosives.) To which I answered no.

Then I remembered that the cab driver had talked about his heart condition. He was on nitrate-pill medication and he had pulled my bag from the trunk of the taxi. Apparently there were traces of nitrates on his hand.

I spent the next 30 minutes filling out forms as TSA officers thoroughly went though my suitcase and attaché case.

Those explosive detection machines are very sensitive.

HOW TO GET HOME WHEN DISASTER STRIKES
--Paul Eisenberg, FOXNews.com.

If the airspace is closed and planes are grounded you have a choice: get stuck, or find another way out. Plan now and have phone numbers ready.
http://fxn.ws/eOKQut

B. Security on the Plane

AIR MARSHALS
In 2010, The United States employed 6,000 Federal Air Marshals (FAM).

Your plane may have air marshals aboard whether flying in the U.S. or internationally. It may be a U.S. carrier or international such as El Al.

While passengers often remark that they feel safer knowing that marshals could be aboard, the airlines grumble they are losing high-revenue seats.
http://usat.ly/dh1hhM, http://bit.ly/9lm4ou

C. Security off the Airport

Be alert of the potential for terrorists to attack public transportation systems and other tourist infrastructure. Be aware of your surroundings. Don't avoid travel, but take common-sense precautions to avoid putting yourself in danger.

Abroad, you are much more likely to be the target of a criminal attack than a terrorist attack. Avoid groups of (especially U.S.) tourists. Regular mass transit is OK; a busload of Americans is a more likely target.

Take taxis that are clearly identified as taxis, and avoid tour buses. The tour bus is an obvious target.

Try to blend in. Europeans do not wear shorts except when taking part in sporting events.

TRAVEL WARNINGS AND ALERTS
Before traveling to a new country, check these travel notes.

They cover natural disasters, terrorist attacks, coups, anniversaries of terrorist events, election-related demonstrations or violence, and high-profile events such as international conferences or regional sports events.
http://bit.ly/cfsVRQ, http://bit.ly/ccY7Rv

WITNESSING A "RIOT"
--Dan Poynter, USA.

On a round-the-world itinerary, I worked in Cape Town, South Africa. My room was in the Southern Sun Cape Sun hotel, downtown, on Strand, 16th floor. One day, I was catching up on email when I heard a strange roaring sound from outside.

I went to the window, opened it and looked down. The noise became much louder. Down in the street, all I could see were heads and shoulders. There were so many people, I could not see pavement in the streets or sidewalks. The people were yelling, screaming, and jumping up and down. A man with a bullhorn was haranguing the crowd. Then an open-top, double decker bus came around the corner. It could barely make headway through the crowd. The mob began rocking the bus.

I thought I was a witness to an urban riot and was glad to be safely separated—up 16 floors.

Later I found my assumption was wrong. The South African rugby team had won the 2007 World Cup title and was returning home in triumph.

In South Africa, they take sports seriously.

GLOBAL INCIDENT MAP.
Check your destinations before you travel. This web site isn't just about terrorism. It also includes situations and incidents around the world which happen every day and which you frequently won't hear about on local or National news. In addition to being able to click on an icon to find more information and a link to related news articles, you can scroll down the page to see the most recent news articles, as well as threats and locations by category.

The site is updated every 360 seconds, constantly. Just click on any map icon for full information at any time. See and bookmark
http://www.globalincidentmap.com/home.php

☺ Humor

JERRY SEINFELD ON AIRPORT SECURITY
http://bit.ly/fnk70A

AIRPORT SECURITY
Pilot: I was once standing in the cockpit door at the beginning of the boarding process when a lovely octogenarian with blue hair hobbled on board. In her one hand she balanced herself with a cane, in the other she carried a small brown carry-on.

The lead flight attendant sang out a cheery greeting to her. "Welcome aboard. How are you today?"

"Well, I guess I'm alright now that they let me go," the feisty old girl said with a chuckle and a twinkle in her eye.

I liked her right away and felt consumed with curiosity about her story. Nonchalantly, I followed to remain in earshot as the flight attendant walked her to her seat.

"Let you go? Did someone not want you to come on this trip?" the FA asked as she took her by the elbow and guided her along.

"Guess not. They took me to jail for a while."

"Jail!" The FA's eyebrows shot up. The image of this sweet little old lady in the hoosegow simple would not compute

"I was in line there at the security check, just minding my own business, when this nice policeman with a lovely puppy dog came by. The doggy took a whiff of my bag and just went nuts. They took me down and put me in this little cell. Other nice men came and asked lots of questions. Then they let me go."

Aha, I thought. This sweet little old lady thing is just a disguise. She was up to no good, and the bomb-sniffing canine nailed her. Only she adroitly talked her way out.

"Well, my goodness, what's in the bag?" queried the flight attendant.

"I've been to visit my son. He gives it to me. He gets it free. His company makes it."

"Well, what is it?"

"Oh, I'm sorry. I didn't say, did I? It's for my puppy at home. My son's company makes dog food."

AUSTRALIAN AIRPORT SECURITY
Underdaks commercial. Video humor. See http://bit.ly/ihTK5i, http://bit.ly/hKVaGz

Chapter Five
Airlines

A. Airlines & Ratings
B. Airline Alliances
C. Loyalty Programs
D. Airline Speak
IATA Codes for airlines, airports, meals, time zones, etc.

A. Airlines & Ratings

FACTOIDS
190,000 commercial airline flights occur in the United States each day.

A new Boeing 777 costs more than $165-million. The expensive engines are installed last.

As an aircraft ascends, the fuselage expands. The air inside is at a greater pressure than the air outside.

Most commercial airliners fly at about 560-mph/901 kmh. This is Mach .80-.86; just below the speed of sound.

Worldwide, commercial airliners use some 5% of the fossil fuels.

Planes burn less fuel at higher altitudes because the air is thinner; there is less friction.

Some airlines buff the aluminum skin of their planes and use a minimum of paint. Paint can weigh up to 1,000-lbs/453 kg, depending on coverage and aircraft size.

More than 235,000 airplanes are registered in the U.S.

In 2009, 704 million domestic and international passengers flew on U.S. airlines

The A-380 can carry 853 passengers in an all-economy configuration, but most airlines fly around 550 passengers in first, business, and economy classes.

Airplanes carry some 40% of the world's cargo.

As of the end of 2008, there were 613,746 active certificated pilots in the U.S. 6% were female.
146,838 pilots had Airline Transport Ratings (ATP) and 124,746 had Commercial Ratings.

For the third consecutive year, Southwest Airlines carried more domestic passengers than any other U.S. carrier. It was the only airline to carry more than 100 million passengers in 2009.

Business Class flyers average more than 18 trips annually in the U.S.

The average age of airline captains has been increasing at U.S. airlines. In 1990, the average age was 43.6; in 2009, it was 48.9—up 12 percent.

In the U.S., airlines employ 60,900 pilots, or 11 pilots per aircraft in operation.

FLYING INCREASES 25% IN TEN YEARS
Air travel saw a significant increase from 2000 to 2009.

The number of scheduled flights by the world's airlines increased by 25% – 59 million to 74 million. And passengers carried 32% – 3.5 billion to more than 4.7 billion.
http://bit.ly/cg3Zcl

FLYING IS THE SAFEST FORM OF TRAVEL
According to the U.S. National Safety Council, you're more likely to die as a pedestrian, on a motorcycle, in a car, on a bus, riding an animal or animal-drawn vehicle, on a train, on a streetcar or on watercraft.
http://bit.ly/gz8BFa

AIRCRAFT ACCIDENT RATE DROPS IN 2009
The International Air Transport Association (IATA) announced the aviation safety performance for 2009 showing that the year's accident rate for Western-built jet aircraft as the second lowest in aviation history.

The 2009 global accident rate was 0.71. That is equal to one accident for every 1.4 million flights.
http://bit.ly/b2VCx8

DIRECTORY OF AIRLINE WEBSITES
The URLS for more than 525 airlines.
http://www.travel-watch.com/airlink.htm

FOLLOW AIRLINES ON TWITTER

Following the various airlines on twitter can give you updates on issues or problems that may affect your travel plans. Read real-time reports from airlines and their passengers.

Add the airlines you use to your Twitter account.

@AlaskaAir - Alaska Airlines
@AmericanAir – American Airlines
@BritishAirways – British Airways
@Continental – Continental Airlines
@Delta – Delta Airlines
@flyfrontier – Frontier Airlines
@JetBlue – JetBlue Airlines
@HawaiianAir – Hawaiian Airlines
@SouthwestAir – Southwest Airlines
@SpiritAirlines – Spirit Airlines
@UnitedAirlines – United Airlines
@USAirways – USAirways
@VirginAmerica – Virgin Airlines
@VirginAtlantic – Virgin Atlantic
http://travelingmamas.com/airlines-on-twitter/

DELTA SHOWS HOW TO USE TWITTER IN A CRISIS

The Christmas time meltdown of the air transport system in the East Coast of the US was driven by the coldest weather in more than 60 years. Twitter to the rescue. See http://bit.ly/gLQfet

✈ **FLYERTALK APP**
FlyerTalk is a forum for the frequent flyer community. Threads debate every possible aspect of being a passenger on commercial airlines. At FT, you can discuss the latest changes made by the airlines and get up-to-date information on air travel.

The "app" is free of charge and works with all Apple devices running iOS 3.2 and higher, which includes the iPad, iPhone 3G/3GS, iPod Touch and iPhone 4. See the App Store.

AIRLINE CODES
There are two character codes from IATA and three-character codes from ICAO.

United is UA and UAL, Lufthansa is LH and DLH, Air Canada is AC and ACA. See the list at http://en.wikipedia.org/wiki/Airline_codes

AIRLINES RATED BY SIZE
Number of passengers carried, tons of cargo flown, etc. See http://www.tetracom.ca/transtalk/?p=1979

THE BUSIEST AIRLINES
Here is a list of top 15 airlines based on Scheduled Passenger-Kilometers Flown. http://bit.ly/b3xR6i

LARGEST INTERNATIONAL AIRLINES
2011. Emirates overtook Lufthansa last year as the largest carrier on international flights, thanks to a six fold increase in traffic since 2000, when it ranked

24th. British Airways, top in 2000, now stands fourth in the International Air Transport Association ranking.
http://bit.ly/cScdlq

SIX AIRLINES RATED FIVE STARS
Asiana, Kingfisher, Qatar, Cathy Pacific, Malaysia, and Singapore.
See the rest of the rankings at
http://bit.ly/ckotwi

ZAGAT'S 2009 AIRLINE SURVEY RATES AIRLINES & AIRPORTS
Continental, JetBlue and Singapore continue to fly high; Southwest named best (U.S.) domestic Value; Virgin America top midsize airline website; Portland (PDX) named top airport, LaGuardia worst.

The survey covers 16 domestic and 73 international airlines, as well as 30 domestic airports. It incorporates the opinions of 5,895 frequent fliers and travel professionals (e.g. travel agents) who collectively took 97,600 flights in the past year.
http://bit.ly/aaGb3T

***GLOBAL TRAVELER* PICKS TOP AIRLINES, HOTELS, ETC.**
Global Traveler Magazine has come out with its annual "GT Tested" reader awards and, as usual, non-U.S. carriers dominate the airline list.

Singapore Airlines was named best airline in the world, Emirates had the best first class, and British

Airways had the best business class. Also ranked are hotels, clubrooms, airports and more.
http://bit.ly/bVsza3

TOP THREE AIRLINES, HOTELS, ETC. WORLDWIDE
See the top-rated travel services in more than 30 categories.
http://dailyqi.com/?p=13503

THE BEST AND WORST INTERNATIONAL CARRIERS
Airlines compared. See
http://bit.ly/bwCWR4

LIST REVEALS WORLD'S DEADLIEST AIRLINES
Aeroflot (Russia) had the highest death total per operator of all commercial airlines, with a total of 8,231 fatalities. Air France ranked second with 1,783 passenger deaths in its history.
See details and the complete list. http://bit.ly/ccBSlB

EU PUBLISHES AIRLINE BLACKLIST
The list includes airlines from Indonesia, the Democratic Republic of Congo, and Sierra Leone.
http://bbc.in/hfjvEp

EUROPEAN COMMISSION UPDATES THE LIST OF AIRLINES BANNED FROM EUROPEAN AIRSPACE
Airlines you should avoid. Several airlines have failed safety inspections by the Commission.
http://bit.ly/h7fxy7. http://bit.ly/gmZeCp

FLYING IN AFGANISTAN

Safi Airways, a start-up Afghan airline, ventures where few air carriers dare to go. Its in-flight magazine tells the ugly truth about the place where you're about to land.

In the seat pocket in front of you on Safi, you will find an article on Kabul heroin addicts, photos of bullet-pocked tourist sites and ads for mine-resistant sport-utility vehicles.

The airline provides this insider's tip about one of the city's leading luxury hotels: "The rooms are individually air-conditioned, accessorized with amenities you will find in 4-star hotels abroad, sheets are clean, view from the room is nice, and—after the suicide bombing that took place—security measures have been implemented."
http://bit.ly/91xJ3o

THE BLACK BOX

David Warren, inventor of the airline "black box," died recently at 85. The Australian scientist came up with the concept of crash-proof and fireproof devices to record flight-deck conversations and instrument data after a 1953 crash involving the Comet, the world's first commercial passenger jet. He created the first prototype of a "black box" in 1956.

20 REASONS TO HATE THE AIRLINES

A brief history of the industry's 30-year campaign to nickel-and-dime us nearly to death
http://bit.ly/cZUSLd

BEST TIME OF THE MONTH TO FLY
Peter Greenberg shares tips on how to prevent possible glitches in your travel experience. Here, he talks about how airlines can run out of crew to fly planes by the end of the month.
http://bit.ly/ficvoT

TEN FLIGHTS THAT ALMOST NEVER ARRIVE ON TIME
Flights to avoid. The most-delayed flights in the US leave passengers waiting and waiting. Anybody booking a ticket on one of these trips is almost certainly guaranteed a late arrival.

See the list:
http://abcnews.go.com/print?id=10849246

SIX WAYS TO SAVE ON FLYING
Alternative airports, re-routing, and buying at the right time.
Why you should call the airline to ask for the "positioning flight."

A video with Peter Greenberg.
http://bit.ly/fveeKS

MORE WAYS TO SAVE
http://bit.ly/dXpi8R

SECRET FLIGHTS
Peter Greenberg video on international flights by major carriers that are not published.
http://bit.ly/hspIdB

TICKET CHANGE FEES

U.S. airlines in the second quarter of 2010 received $593.6 million USD in revenue from fees charged to passengers canceling or changing reservations, the U.S. Department of Transportation reports.

http://bit.ly/fXawUh

AIRLINERS.NET

All about commercial aviation.

http://www.airliners.net/

TWENTY MOST POPULAR AIRLINE ROUTES

Hong Kong -- Taipei is number one.
Followed by Los Angeles to New York and New York to London.

http://bit.ly/9vrgIm

2010 WORLD AIRLINE AWARD WINNERS ANNOUNCED

--Joe Sherren, Canada.

Asiana Airlines wins the Skytrax Airline of the Year 2010 title, Singapore Airlines (2nd) and Qatar Airways 3rd. These Awards are known and respected around the world as the Passenger's Choice Awards

The 2010 World Airline Award winners include:

Air Arabia, Air Asia, Air Berlin, Air Canada, Air New Zealand, Asiana Airlines, Cathay Pacific, Dragonair, Emirates, Etihad Airways, Finnair, Garuda Indonesia, GOL, Hainan Airlines, IndiGo, Kingfisher Airlines, Kulula, LAN Airlines,

Lufthansa, Malaysia Airlines, Malev Hungarian Airlines, Oneworld, Qantas Airways, Qatar Airways, Singapore Airlines, South African Airways, Swiss Int'l Airlines, TACA Airlines, Thai Airways, Thomson Airways, Turkish Airlines, Virgin America, Virgin Atlantic, Virgin Blue, WestJet
http://www.worldairlineawards.com/

AIRLINER HYPERMILING SAVES FUEL

During a transatlantic flight, an airliner typically is assigned a fairly limited track of airspace to follow to its destination. It's like flying through a narrow pipeline. On United's demonstration flight, pilots were assigned a flexible track—in essence, a bigger pipeline. The wider swath allowed the pilots to wander a bit, going where the best winds will help push the plane along. Or, in the case of a headwind, minimize the resistance.

Airlines already know, based upon forecasts and information from other aircraft, where to find the best winds. But pilots are forced to follow the narrow track over the ocean because vast swaths of the sea are not covered by radar.
http://bit.ly/a3H81N
http://bit.ly/cL1jVV

WHO IS FLYING THE PLANE BESIDES THE PILOT?

There are a lot of other people working behind the scenes.
http://bit.ly/bLtaCz

AIR TRAVEL CONSUMER REPORT—U.S.
Get the numbers on flight delays, mishandled baggage, consumer complaints, etc. Read what airlines do when you complain
http://bit.ly/f8FOGB

AIRLINE SAFETY AND SECURITY INFORMATION
This site is your source for plane crashes involving passenger airliners, as well as other, airline safety and aviation safety information, such as accident statistics, aircraft safety changes, and aviation safety and accident investigation news. Here you can also find information on TSA restrictions, passenger-screening procedures at airports, and other airport security information. In addition, they offer extensive fear of flying resources, lists of air travel tips, and access to a wide range of safety databases and accident statistics from the NTSB and elsewhere.
http://www.airsafe.com/

PILOT SHORTAGE AHEAD
The shortage of commercial pilots globally is expected to be significant in the next decade. Currently global pilot training programs can train only about 15,000 per year, which would leave a shortfall of more than 3,000 new pilots annually.
http://bit.ly/d3GwOC
http://bit.ly/duwsIa
http://bit.ly/9S9D7E

UNITED AIRLINES FOUNDATION

The United Airlines Foundation provides financial support to organizations focused on education, arts & culture, health & youth initiatives and engages employees and customers in many related programs. Since its inception in 1952, the Foundation has touched countless lives directly and has inspired thousands of employees, customers and community members to explore and address issues that affect them personally.

For grant guidelines and a list of grantees, see http://bit.ly/gWii7J

AMERICAN AIRLINES HAS AN APP

An air travel app that understands who you are and where you're going. From the airport you're departing and from what gate.

Where you'll sit and even where you are on the standby list.

Simply swipe and tap your way through your personalized American Airlines travel information with the app that's perfect for flying through airports.

Download free from the iPhone App Store.
http://bit.ly/b2huMh

PLANE FINDER iPHONE APP

Plane Finder lets iPhone users point their phones at the sky to see data about flights passing overhead.

Among the data presented to users: How fast the planes are moving, where they're going, where they started, their altitude, the flight number and how far the aircraft is from the person's smartphone at exactly that moment.

To accomplish this, the app employs "augmented reality" technology, which refers to an emerging--and at times clunky--category of smartphone apps that seek to overlay digital information on top of the real world.

Augmented reality apps let people essentially use their phones as a lens through which to view what's going on around them. The apps switch phones into camera mode, so users see a moving picture of the nearby environment. Then they take data from the Internet and plot it on top of the picture.

See
http://bit.ly/cw8Rga
And the App Store.
Some people recommend you test the free version first.

FLIGHT NUMBERS
Flight numbers are assigned by the airlines. The lower numbers are often given to the longer, more prestigious flights. An example might be UA-001.

FLIGHT TERMINOLOGY
Nonstop, connecting, through or direct?

A "connecting flight" makes stops and plane changes.

A "through flight" makes stops, a plane change and an airline change.
A "direct flight" may make stops without a plane or airline change.
A "nonstop flight" does not make stops.

Airline websites may not be clear on stops, plane, and airline changes. Ask.

PHONETIC ALPHABET
The military and the airline industry use a phonetic alphabet to be understood. If you call your airline and use these terms, you may sound like a frequent flyer that knows what you are doing.

A - Alpha
B - Bravo
C - Charlie
D - Delta
E - Echo
F - Foxtrot
G - Golf
H - Hotel
I - India
J - Juliet
K - Kilo
L - Lima
M - Mike
N - November
O - Oscar
P - Papa
Q - Quebec
R - Romeo
S - Sierra

T - Tango
U - Uniform
V - Victor
W - Whiskey
X - X-ray
Y – Yankee
Z - Zulu
http://bit.ly/gjtvX9

LONGEST COMMERCIAL FLIGHTS
Considering distance.

Time can be affected by the Jet Stream, winds, and ATC routing.

EWR-SIN is the longest at 18 hrs 50 mins (Singapore Airlines)

Followed by:
LAX-SIN (Singapore Airlines)
ATL-JNB (Delta)
DXB-LAX (Emirates)
BKK-LAX (Thai)
DXB-IAH (Emirates)
DXB-SFO (Emirates)
JFK - HKG (Cathay)
EWR-HKG (Continental)
DOH-IAH (Qatar)
http://en.wikipedia.org/wiki/Non-stop_flight

THE TOP TEN (PLUS ONE) THINGS YOU WISH AIRLINES WOULD DO TO MAKE YOUR TRIP GO A LITTLE SMOOTHER

Such as provide a "family" section in Economy to keep the kids in the same area. See more at http://bit.ly/fswcUg

PLANE LAVATORIES

The first toilets in airplanes were simple buckets. Aircraft cabins were not pressurized and it was easy to open doors and windows.

Read the history of airplane toilets and some good guidelines for their use.
http://asiaspirit.com/lavatory.html

FACTOID

SAS installed seatback mirrors on some jets to so passengers can check their appearance without having to go to the **lavatory**.

OPENING A LOCKED LAVATORY

Flight attendants often lock lavatory doors during turbulence, takeoff, and landing. The door sign will show red dot or an "occupied" sign.

Sometimes after takeoff, they forget to unlock the doors.

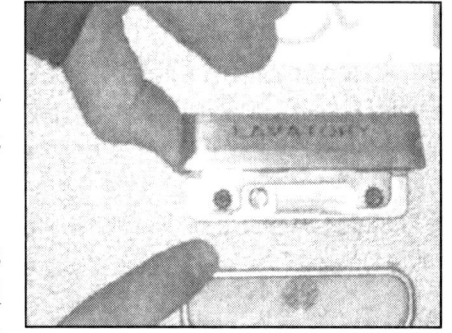

Some lavatory locks have a small vertical slot you can slide

sideways with a key. Others have a cover you can lift to expose a sliding latch.

Do not do this if there is any chance someone might be in the lavatory.

AIRLINES CHARGING FOR TOILET USE?
Video. http://aol.it/cgIaSG

FACTOID
Coach passengers often share the toilet with 45 others. First class with 10 others. These numbers are increasing.

Aircraft toilets use about 8 oz/.24 L of water per flush. Water has weight. Airlines want to carry as little as possible.

B. Airline Alliances

FAVOR ONE CARRIER
It pays to favor one airline for its award programs and alliances. Building points with one carrier will produce more upgrades, boarding preferences, etc.

When flying a partner airline, mention on check-in that your points (miles) should go to your home-airline account.

Most air carriers also issue a branded credit card. They credit you with points for the money you spend. This is "double dipping" on miles and builds points faster.

AIRLINE WORLD ALLIANCES

Airlines of the world have linked together to offer easier ticket purchasing and connections to the global traveler. Here are the other airlines your favorite carrier is connected with.

http://bit.ly/cpFcOK

--Star Alliance: United Airlines/Continental, Lufthansa, SAS, Air Canada, Varig, Thai Airways, All Nippon Airways, Air New Zealand, Singapore Airlines, Mexicana Airlines, Austrian Airlines, BMI, Croatia, South African, Spanair, Adria, Asiana, SWISS, EgyptAir, LOT, TAP, Turkish, Air China, Scandinavian, Blue 1, ANA, US Airways, Avianca-TACA and Copa Airlines.

http://www.staralliance.com/en/

--OneWorld: American Airlines, British Airways, Canadian Airlines, Cathay Pacific, Finnair, Iberia, Qantas, Japan Airlines, LAN, Malev, Royal Jordanian, S-7/Globus (Russia).

http://www.oneworld.com/

--SkyTeam: Delta, Air France, Korean, Aeroflot, Aero Mexico, Alitalia, China Southern, KLM, CSA Czech Airlines, Air Europa, Kenya Airways, Aerolíneas Argentinas, Garuda Indonesia.

COMPARING INTERNATIONAL AIRLINE ALLIANCES

Shopping for perks: How do Star Alliance, OneWorld and SkyTeam compare in value to the customer?

See which group of airlines is best for you.

http://bit.ly/a2q7I4

ROUND-THE-WORLD ITINERARIES

Circumnavigating the globe can be fun, inexpensive and results in more airline points. Generally, you must fly one direction (no back-tracking), visit 3-15 countries and the trip can run from a couple of weeks to several months. Distances run from 25,000 to 35,000 miles. See websites for details.
http://www.StarAlliance.com, http://bit.ly/eErUTm
http://www.oneworld.com/

✈ **FLYERTALK FORUM FOR AIRLINE ALLIANCE DISCUSSSIONS**
http://www.flyertalk.com/forum/miles-points-1/

VIDEOS ON AIRLINE ALLIANCES
http://bit.ly/c5F3cH

C. Loyalty ("Frequent Flyers") Programs

FACTOIDS

More than 60-million people in the U.S. are members of a frequent flyer program.

Nearly half of frequent flyer miles are earned on the ground. Some are through hotels, rental cars, restaurants, etc.

Some 75 percent of the earned frequent flyer miles are never redeemed. The airlines count on this.

Frequent flyers earn and use some 12-million tickets annually.

About a quarter of the passengers in First Class are paying full fare. The rest are upgrades and airline employees.

HISTORY OF LOYALTY PROGRAMS
Miles & More, Mileage Plus. AAdvantage, KrisFlyer and others. How it all began. See http://www.frequentflier.com/ffp-005.htm

DIRECT LINKS TO AIRLINES' FREQUENT FLYER WEB PAGES
Compare loyalty programs. See http://www.frequentflier.com/ffp-002.htm

UNDERSTANDING AIRLINE LOYALTY PROGRAMS
Video. http://bit.ly/c5F3cH, http://bit.ly/i3jQDQ

BUSINESS AND LEISURE TRAVELERS DIFFERENT REWARDS
Praveen Kopalle, associate professor of marketing at the Tuck School of Business at Dartmouth, finds that business and leisure travelers prefer different types of rewards programs.

Business flyers prefer tiered loyalty programs that allow them to earn more perks the more they fly (i.e. access to VIP lounges, faster check-in, etc).

Leisure travelers prefer loyalty programs that allow them to earn miles towards free flights.

Kopalle says that airlines should review their loyalty programs to ensure that they are in line with the types of customers they want to attract. For most airlines, it is more financially beneficial to attract a loyal following of business travelers. Video.
http://bit.ly/eKCOl7

GETTING MORE MILES AND USING THEM
Peter Greenberg video about why it is easier than ever to cash in frequent flyer miles.
http://bit.ly/eUq19U

YOU CAN'T ALWAYS GET WHAT YOU WANT
Redeeming airline rewards can be a challenge if you're looking for First- or Business-class seats. Patience and timing are essential.
http://bit.ly/9nUesI, http://www.SeatGuru.com

SPENDING FREQUENT FLIER MILES FOR OTHER THAN SEATS
To lessen mounting traveler frustration over the difficulty of booking frequent-flier tickets, airlines are offering members a cornucopia of goods that have little to do with flights.

Because of the reduction in available seats, some airlines are promoting hotel stays, car rentals, merchandise, and gift cards.

United created an entire ad campaign around alternative-award options and is billing itself as the airline that "wants you to use your miles."
http://nyti.ms/b5lH2k

POINTS.COM
Points.com helps you get the most from your loyalty programs--from your airline frequent flyer miles to your hotel points, from your credit card rewards to your gas station and drugstore cards.

You can get, move, give, or redeem your points, miles, and rewards from many of the world's leading programs. You can manage more than 100 of the top loyalty programs, such as Aeroplan®, American Airlines AAdvantage®, American Express® Membership Rewards®, Airmiles, Delta SkyMiles®, Priority Club® Rewards, US Airways® Dividend Miles® and many more, all from one convenient location.
http://bit.ly/eiXjMe,
http://www.mileagemanager.com/

ORPHAN AIRLINE MILES AND HOTEL POINTS
If you have miles or points in programs that aren't your main ones but don't want to lose them, hotels must have some activity within 12 months and airlines within 18 months, so keep an eye on those accounts.

You don't have to fly them or stay at them to keep your account active. You can make a small purchase at their online store or you can buy a minimum amount of points to deposit into your account.

✈ FLYERTALK FORUM ON LOYALTY PROGRAMS
MilesBuzz!
Discussion of the latest frequent flyer program buzz.
http://www.flyertalk.com/forum/miles-points-1/

✈ **FLYERTALK FORUM ON OTHER LOYALTY PROGRAMS/PARTNERS**
Amtrak, etc.
http://www.flyertalk.com/forum/miles-points-1/

✈ **FLYERTALK FORUM ON DISCONTINUED PROGRAMS/PARTNERS**
http://www.flyertalk.com/forum/miles-points-1/

✈ **FLYERTALK FORUM ON SITES WITH POINTS AND ALTERNATIVE MILES**
S.P.A.M. (Sites with Points & Alternative Miles) S.P.A.M., including referral bonuses, congas and any other loyalty currencies.
http://www.flyertalk.com/forum/s-p-m-2/

✈ **UNDERSTANDING THE FLYERTALK FORUM**
Members of FlyerTalk use a lot of abbreviations and acronyms. To understand them, see the Glossary link at the bottom of the Home page.
http://www.FlyerTalk.com

UP IN THE AIR FILM TRAILER
It about getting better treatment when you fly a lot of miles.
George Clooney on frequent flying. Video.
http://bit.ly/glhI19

HIGHEST STATUS AIRLINE PROGRAMS ARE SECRET
Perhaps you saw the *Up In The Air* film with George Clooney. He qualified for the coveted "Black Card" from American Airlines. See
http://bit.ly/h90e9J

Airport lines can be a thing of the past. So are middle seats, waiting on hold when calling customer service and missed connections. Instead, air travel can bring earlier upgrades, first in line for meal choice, early boarding & access to overhead bins, complimentary cocktails, first name greetings and a hidden check-in process. Some airlines have these secret super-elite memberships.

These programs are for the airlines' most valuable customers. There are no published criteria and are by invitation only. Often the carrier takes into consideration the amount you spend on Business and First Class tickets, your opinion-molder standing, your celebrity status, etc. In other words, how much do you spend and are you influential.

Million Milers FLY a lot.
Global Service members SPEND a lot.
http://bit.ly/bgc3pn

These exclusive clubs are named as follows:

United Airlines: Global Services
http://bit.ly/b9ITPR

American Airlines: Concierge Key

Continental: Presidential Platinum Elite
http://bit.ly/9x8gCm

Delta: Executive Partner

For more, search for "Global Service" in this book.

See http://bit.ly/ctg3yN (Click on the video and wait for the ad to play through) It will give you a capsule of the entire 'Up in the air' show in 2:23 minutes.
and
http://bit.ly/axa8vf
and
http://bit.ly/idOu0R (Wait for commercial message).
and
http://bit.ly/9QFaXY

✈ FLYERTALK FORUM ON UNITED GLOBAL SERVICES
http://bit.ly/dAVPgO
Check the posting dates and go to the last page.

MILEAGE RUNS
According to CNN, some people make extra trips to build frequent flyer miles. Lufthansa even charters flights for groups wanting to build their mileage account.
http://bit.ly/9BfahY
http://www.starmegado.com/

✈ FLYERTALK FORUM ON MILEAGE RUNS

Mileage Run Deals
The place to post airfare deals conducive to mileage running, including possible pricing errors and unusually low fares. Note: Weekly or other regularly posted fare sales are generally not considered unusually good deals.
http://bit.ly/glQ8JO

Mileage Run Discussion
Discussion of methods to maximize miles and/or points either through trips dedicated to no other reason than the miles/points, or through creative alteration of trips to extend their earning capacity in often-unique ways.
http://bit.ly/hlYhvV

D. Airline Speak Glossaries

AIR TRAVEL LINGO
Here is some of the terminology used by pilots, flight attendants, gate agents, security personnel, et. al. with each other. You can sound like a pro with these words and acronyms used in the airline and travel industry.

ABA: Able Bodied Assistant. Person traveling with a disabled person.
Blue Juice: The water in the toilet on some smaller and/or older planes.
Coat-Switch Room: The lost-and-found.
Codesharing: When one airline provides service under another carrier's name. Both airlines' codes appear in reservation systems, flight video monitors and on tickets. Codeshare flights often accrue mileage if you specify which airline program you want your points to go to at check-in.
Conga Line: A FlyerTalk thread in which members help each other by lending their referrals for a select promotion. Most promotions that offer a bonus for referring a friend will have a corresponding Conga Line thread on http://www.flyertalk.com/

Crotch Watch: Flight attendants checking to make sure passengers have their seat belts fastened when the Fasten Seat Belt light comes on. Also: "groin scan."
Crumb Crunchers: Babies, children, young kids. Called "rug rats" at home.
Deadheading: A return flight made by a commercial aircraft without any cargo or paying passengers on board. Also commonly used when an airline employee flies as a passenger to get home or to work.
DBC: Denied Boarding Compensation. May be a later flight, a "free" ticket and/or money. See IDB.
The D**k-Measuring Device: What some TSA officers call the Back-Scatter Imaging machine at Security.
DM List: Departure Management list. Used by airlines at gate to determine and allocate upgrades.
Drink Chits: A coupon valid for one free (or prepaid) alcoholic beverage on that airline's flight. The coupon may sometimes be valid in an airport lounge.
E+: United's "Economy Plus" section with extra legroom.
E-: The remainder of the United Economy section after E+ rows.
Equipment. Airplanes. When you don't see your plane at the gate, don't ask the agent if the flight is on time. Ask, "Where's the equipment that's due to operate my flight?" That will force the agent to go to the computer and find out where your aircraft is and when it will actually arrive.
ETA: Estimated Time of Arrival.
F/O: First Officer, a.k.a. Co-Pilot
FA: Flight Attendant

Gate Lice: The passengers who congregate near the boarding gate so they can be one of the early boarders. (To find storage area for their carry-ons.)
Gateway Airports: Domestic airports that are origination points for foreign destinations.
George: The autopilot. As when the pilot says "I'll let George take over."
GIB. Gate Information-display Board. The monitors near each gate that provides seating, departure and other flight-specific information.
IDB: Involuntarily Denied Boarding. Airline usually offers cash consolation.
Jim Wilson: A dead passenger being transported in the cargo area.
Landing Lips: Female passengers when they put on their lipstick just before landing.
Lap Children. Babies younger than two not required to pay for a seat. They should be held the entire flight.
Left Seat: Where the captain sits.
Load. Looking for an upgrade? Don't blindly inquire about your chances. Ask, "How are the loads today?" The agent will tell you how many seats are empty and your number on the upgrade wait list.
Matron: Airline employee, often a middle-aged woman, who polices access to business and first class lounges.
Metal: Refers to aircraft you are flying. (i.e., United metal, American metal, etc.)
Mileage Run: A series of flights taken in a very short amount of time, solely for the purpose of accumulating frequent flyer miles, with a blatant disregard for the destinations.

Op-up: Short for operational upgrade. A type of upgrade that is awarded when coach is overbooked and they bump some passengers up to business or first class if there are any seats open. The pecking order starts with top elite members, etc.
PBM: Positive bag matching. Aircraft will not leave unless all passengers checking bags are on board.
Pax: Shorthand for passengers.
PNR: Passenger Name Record. Used to record reservation and passenger information.
Predepartures. What flight attendants call the drinks that are served before takeoff to passengers seated in business and first class.
Pushback: When the plane leaves the gate. If the plane is already at the gate, ask, "When are we scheduled to push back?"
The pushback could be a very short distance but is when the door is closed, the jetway is pulled back, and the plane rolls back. The time is recorded as the (on-time) departure time.
Right Seat: Where the Co-Pilot sits.
RT: Round Trip.
RTW: Round the World ticket package.
Segment: A section or "leg" of a continuous itinerary.
SLF: Flight crew lingo for Passengers: Self Loading Freight.
Passengers or PAX.
Spinners: Late boarding passengers who don't have a seat assignment. They are spinning around looking for a seat.
Squawks: Problem listings that pilots leave for maintenance crews to fix before the next flight.

SSSS: Selected for Secondary Security Screening. Randomly printed on the bottom of boarding passes. Allocate more time for Security.
T/O: Take off.
Tappian: The refilling of plastic water bottles with airplane tap water.
Two-for-one special: The aircraft bounces twice on landing.
Upgrade: e.g., being moved up from Economy Class to First Class seating. Sometimes call "uplift" in the UK.
VDB: Voluntary denied boarding. More commonly known as a "bump." Most airlines offer money, travel credits or "VDB vouchers" in such instances. Make sure the ticket offered can be used any time. Some are space-available tickets.
Wheels up. When the plane is flying. If the wheels are retracted any sooner, the pilot is sure to be demoted.
Working the Village: Flight attendants assigned to the Economy section.
Working the Wall: The Customer Service Counter on the concourse. The "Wall" is where travelers go when there is a problem with their itinerary. The distressed travelers are often screaming and yelling and wailing.

How do you learn the jargon? Listen to how airline employees talk to each other. Use it properly and employees will assume you know more than you really do—and they'll respond with more information than they volunteer to average fliers. See more air lingo at
http://pilots4rent.com/avlan.shtml

PODIUM OR COUNTER?
It is not likely you will ever see a "podium" at an airport. A podium is a platform raised above the surrounding level to give prominence to the person on it. Yet you hear references to a podium constantly. Airline employees are referring to a counter.
http://bit.ly/dDwKPd

"WATER LANDINGS"
The only planes that make water landings are amphibians and float planes. Wheeled planes don't *land* in the water, they *crash* into the water.

IATA CODES
For Airlines, Airports, Meals, Time Zones, Etc.

IATA codes are abbreviations that the International Air Transport Association (IATA) publishes to facilitate air travel. They are typically 1-, 2-, 3-, or 4-character combinations (referred to as unigrams, digrams, trigrams, or tetragrams, respectively) that uniquely identify locations, equipment, companies, and times to standardize international flight operations. All codes within each group follow a pattern (same number of characters, and using either all letters or letter/digit combinations) to reduce the potential for error.

       1 Airport codes
       2 Airline designators
       3 Aircraft type designators
       4 Country codes
       5 Currency codes

6 IATA time zone codes
7 IATA region codes
8 IATA meal codes
9 IATA class codes
http://bit.ly/gu8TX9

AIRPORT, AIRLINE AND AIRCRAFT CODE DATABASES
http://bit.ly/cGWwM2
http://www.atlasnavigator.com/dictionary.html
http://bit.ly/h2qX96
http://bit.ly/e4QJ12
http://www.onetravel.com/travel/glossary.asp
http://www.travelyucatan.com/glossary.htm
http://airodyssey.net/reference/glossary/

✈ **Terms used by frequent flyers on FlyerTalk**
http://www.flyertalk.com/glossary/

☺ Humor

OXYMORA ON AIR TRAVEL
"Your coat has been **found** . . . **missing**.
"Your request for an upgrade was **clearly** . . . **misunderstood**."
"This airline supplies **plastic** . . . **silverware**."
" On the plane, the microwaved omelet is your **only** . . . **choice**"
" Your last trip was a **working** . . . **holiday**"
" Your missing bag is a **minor** . . . **crisis**"
"I could go on and on. **Good** . . . **grief**"

AIRPLANE MAINTENANCE

"Squawks" are problem listings that pilots generally leave for maintenance crews to fix before the next flight. Here are some squawks submitted by pilots and the replies from the maintenance crews.

(P) = Problem (S) = Solution

(P) Left inside main tire almost needs replacement
(S) Almost replaced left inside main tire

(P) Test flight OK, except autoland very rough
(S) Autoland not installed on this aircraft

(P) #2 Propeller seeping prop fluid
(S) #2 Propeller seepage normal - #1 #3 and #4 propellers lack normal seepage

(P) Something loose in cockpit
(S) Something tightened in cockpit

(P) Evidence of leak on right main landing gear
(S) Evidence removed

(P) DME volume unbelievably loud
(S) Volume set to more believable level

(P) Dead bugs on windshield
(S) Live bugs on order

(P) Autopilot in altitude hold mode produces a 200 fpm decent
(S) Cannot reproduce problem on ground

(P) Friction locks cause throttle levers to stick
(S) That's what they're there for

(P) Number three engine missing
(S) Engine found on right wing after brief search

(P) Aircraft handles funny
(S) Aircraft warned to straighten up, "fly right," and be serious

(P) Target Radar hums
(S) Reprogrammed Target Radar with the lyrics

GEAR PINS INSTALLED

While taxiing out in sequence behind a Lufthansa airliner at Frankfurt, a C-130 Hercules crew noticed an orange "Remove before flight" streamer hanging out of the Lufthansa nose wheel well (their nose gear locking pin was still installed).

Not wanting to cause too much embarrassment by going through the controller, the 130 crew simply called the Lufthansa aircraft on the tower frequency: "Lufthansa aircraft, Herky 23." No reply.

They repeated the transmission and again there was no reply. Instead, the Lufthansa pilot called the tower and asked the tower to tell the Herky crew that "the professional pilots of Lufthansa do not engage in unprofessional conversations over the radio."

The 130 pilot quickly replied, "Frankfurt tower, can you please relay to the professional pilots of the

Lufthansa aircraft that their nose gear pin is still installed?"

EDUCATION
Remember it takes a college degree to fly a plane, but only a high school diploma to fix one.

THE FLYING CLUB'S CESSNA 172
The Air Canada Employee Flying Club was extremely proud the day the four-seater Cessna 172, newly painted in the airline's colors, was rolled out of the hangar for the first time.

It was tiny in comparison to other planes at the Toronto Maintenance Base, and flying it made for some interesting radio exchanges.

"Toronto Ground, this is Allegheny 357. I'd like taxi clearance."
Ground Control: "Roger, Allegheny.... Hold short, you have an Air Canada L-1011, an Air Canada DC-8 and an Air Canada Cessna 172 passing in front."

Allegheny: "Well, I'll be . . . papa bear, mama bear and the iddy biddy baby bear."

THE HEAVY AND THE ITTY-BITSY AIRPLANE
One day the pilot of a Cherokee 180 was told by the tower to hold short of the active runway while a DC-8 landed.

The DC-8 landed, rolled out turned around, and taxied back past the Cherokee.

Some quick-witted comedian in the DC-8 crew got on the radio and said, "What a cute little plane. Did you make it all by yourself?"

The Cherokee pilot, not about to let the insult go by, came back with a real zinger: "I made it out of DC-8 parts.

Another landing like yours and I'll have enough parts for another one."

DEAN MARTIN & FOSTER BROOKS
Dean Martin and the Amazing Foster Brooks chat in a Bar. A true video classic. http://bit.ly/gtPkAD

DAVID LETTERMAN'S TOP TEN LIST
Signs Your Airline is About to go Bankrupt
See http://bit.ly/fjsIEC

DAVID LETTERMAN TOP TEN LIST
Airlines & Pilots
See http://bit.ly/dM2muf

TROUBLE WITH PLANE ENGINES
While cruising at 36,000 feet, the airplane shuddered, and a passenger looked out the window.

"Oh no!" he screamed, "One of the engines just blew up!"

Other passengers left their seats and came running over; suddenly the aircraft was rocked by a second blast as yet another engine exploded on the other side.

The passengers were in a panic now, and even the flight attendant couldn't maintain order. Just then, standing tall and smiling confidently, the pilot strode from the cockpit and assured everyone that there was nothing to worry about. His words and his demeanor made most of the passengers feel better, and they sat down as the pilot calmly walked to the door of the aircraft. There, he grabbed several packages from under the seats and began handing them to the flight attendants.

Each crewmember attached the package to their backs.

"Say," spoke up an alert passenger, "Aren't those parachutes?"

The pilot confirmed that they were.

The passenger went on, "But I thought you said there was nothing to worry about?"

"There isn't," replied the pilot as a third engine exploded. "We're going to get help."

FLIGHT SAFETY
A friend of mine was learning how to fly (a plane, obviously) and asked his instructor the safety benefits of a twin-engine aircraft.

His reply: "If one engine fails, the other takes you to the scene of the accident."

LIGHTS

During emergency-landing training, I asked my flight instructor how to handle a night emergency.

He said, "Same way. Set up for maximum glide as you look for a place to set it down. Just before you land, turn on your landing light. If you like what you see, go ahead and land.
If you don't like what you see, turn off the landing lights."

THINGS WHICH DO YOU NO GOOD IN AVIATION

- ✈ Altitude above you.
- ✈ Runway behind you.
- ✈ Fuel in the truck.
- ✈ Half a second in history.
- ✈ Approach plates in the car.
- ✈ The airspeed you don't have.

RULES OF THE AIR FOR PILOTS

An airplane will probably fly a little bit over gross (weight), but it won't fly without fuel.

Speed is life, altitude is life insurance.

Too many pilots are found in the wreckage with their hands around a microphone or holding onto a keyboard. Don't drop the aircraft in order to fly the microphone.

An airplane flies because of a principle discovered by Bernoulli, not Marconi.

Fly it until the last piece stops moving.

Any attempt to stretch fuel is guaranteed to increase headwinds.

A thunderstorm is nature's way of saying "Up yours."

Keep looking around, there's always something you missed.

Remember, you're always a student in an airplane.

Any pilot who does not at least privately consider himself the best in the business is in the wrong business.

Helicopters can't fly; they're just so ugly the earth repels them.

Hovering (helicopters) is for pilots who love to fly, but have no place to go.

The only time you have too much fuel is when you're on fire.

The only thing worse than a captain who never flew copilot is a copilot who was once a captain.

A "terminal forecast" is a horoscope with numbers.

The first thing every pilot does after making a gear-up landing is to put the gear handle down.

A good simulator check ride is like successful surgery on a cadaver.

A smooth touchdown in a simulator is about as exciting as kissing your sister.

An airplane may disappoint a good pilot, but it won't surprise him.
Learn from the mistakes of others. You won't live long enough to make them all yourself.

Three things kill young pilots in Alaska: weather, weather, and weather.

Any Captain who takes less than 45 minutes of holding fuel is playing Russian Roulette with the ground.

Every takeoff is optional. Every landing is mandatory.

If you push the stick forward, the houses get bigger. If you pull the stick back, they get smaller. That is, unless you keep pulling the stick all the way back, then they get bigger again.

Flying isn't dangerous. Crashing is what's dangerous.

It's always better to be down here wishing you were up there than up there wishing you were down here.

The ONLY time you have too much fuel is when you're on fire.

The propeller is just a big fan in front of the plane used to keep the pilot cool. When it stops, you can actually watch the pilot start sweating.

When in doubt, hold on to your altitude. No one has ever collided with the sky.

A 'good' landing is one from which you can walk away. A 'great' landing is one after which they can use the plane again.

You know you've landed with the wheels up if it takes full power to taxi to the ramp.

The probability of survival is inversely proportional to the angle of arrival. Large angle of arrival, small probability of survival and vice versa.

Never let an aircraft take you somewhere your brain didn't get to five minutes earlier.

Stay out of clouds. The silver lining everyone keeps talking about might be another airplane going in the opposite direction. Reliable sources also report that mountains have been known to hide out in clouds.

There are three simple rules for making a smooth landing. Unfortunately no one knows what they are.

You start with a bag full of luck and an empty bag of experience. The trick is to fill the bag of experience before you empty the bag of luck.

If all you can see out of the window is ground that's going round and round and all you can hear is commotion coming from the passenger compartment, things are not at all as they should be.

In the ongoing battle between objects made of aluminum going hundreds of miles per hour and the ground going zero miles per hour, the ground has yet to lose.

Good judgment comes from experience. Unfortunately, the experience usually comes from bad judgment.

It's always a good idea to keep the pointy end going forward and the dirty side down.

Remember, gravity is not just a good idea. It's the law. And it's not subject to repeal.

The three most useless things to a pilot are the altitude above you, runway behind you, and a tenth of a second ago.

BASIC FLYING RULES FOR PILOTS

1. Try to stay in the middle of the air.

2. Do not go near the edges of it.
3. The edges of the air can be recognized by the appearance of ground, buildings, sea, trees, and interstellar space.

It is much more difficult to fly in the edges.

BOEING 747 DRAG RACE (Video)
http://bit.ly/fu92Ie

DEFINITION OF A HELICOPTER
Thousands of barely-connected parts revolving around an oil leak.

Chapter Six
Air Traffic Control

FACTOIDS
Control tower windows are tilted 15%-out at the top to reduce reflections.

There are three million flights through UK airspace every year.

Some 61-million people are in the air above the U.S. at any one time.

O'Hare (ORD) controllers handle 210 flights per hour during peak periods.

27,000 flights take off in the U.S. each day.

Passengers flown last year on scheduled U.S. airlines: 769.4 million.

AIR TRAFFIC MANAGEMENT GLOSSARY OF TERMS.
From AAR to ZTL. See http://bit.ly/a7LIgY

WORLD AIR TRAFFIC
View From Satellite
Read the text before playing the video. It is a 24-hour observation of all of the large aircraft flights in the world, condensed down to about 2 minutes. Note the sunlight movement and the preponderance of planes flying west during the day and east after

dark. Also note the amount of traffic across the North Atlantic.
http://bit.ly/i92EEk

NEW TECHNOLOGIES THAT WOULD MAKE THE LIFE OF A TRAVELING CONSULTANT EASIER
--Joe Sherren, Canada.

There are always cool new technologies that consultants can use. Many are ones that are fascinating but you probably could never find a good time and place to use them. Here, however, is one that frequent airline travelers can use. It is called Flightaware.

Say you are waiting for a flight to arrive and the arrival board is telling you the flight is on time, but there seem to be lots of other delayed flights. Want to know exactly what is going on with your arriving flight?

Go to Flightaware and see "Live Tracking." enter the airport or airline and flight number to see exactly where the flight is, its track over the ground, altitude and speed, and when it will land. There has been more than one time when I have been able to tell the gate agent what is going on with a flight when the airline's own information is out of date.

Tip: Flightaware has the history of each flight for duration, departure, and arrival. This will give you some information on how likely your flight is to be on time. Comments left by users about certain flights

can also be helpful to select flights. This is a good site to bookmark in your favorites on your smart phone so you can always know where your plane is and when it will arrive.
http://flightaware.com/

THE DEPARTURE BOARD IS LYING TO YOU
Compare it with the arrivals board.
A Peter Greenberg video. http://bit.ly/hG08G7

SKYbrary
Resource for aviation knowledge.
http://www.skybrary.aero/landingpage/

WHAT IS GOING ON IN THE AIR OVER EUROPE?
--Joe Brancatelli, USA.

Eurocontrol, the pan-European air-traffic control system, has been brilliant as an informational source. When there is bad weather in Europe or employees strike airlines, the European Organisation for the Safety of Air Navigation, becomes essential. They ensure that your European flight will be safe, punctual, and sustainable.

See and sign up for this Twitter feed
http://www.twitter.com/eurocontrol

TOUR AN ATC FACILITY
A glimpse of a real air traffic control facility.
Whenever you fly, people like those shown here are watching over you, making sure you arrive safely.

It's a vital profession and, as you will see, requires a lot of concentration, skill, and judgment.
http://bit.ly/fGxZzf

TAKING OFF
Get a look at the view from the 767 cockpit as the plane begins its journey from New York to Los Angeles.
http://www.youtube.com/watch?v=NUlfBt-6EJE

WHAT'S HAPPENING UP FRONT?
See the action in the cockpit of a Virgin Atlantic Boeing 747 from LHR to SFO during takeoff and landing.
http://bit.ly/bJsTf3

LUFTHANSA A340-300 PILOT WANTS TO LEAVE HIS AIRPLANE TO CLOSE A DOOR
While waiting in a long queue for departure at New York's Kennedy airport, a Lufthansa flight crew is alerted to a possible fuel panel door open on the outside of the fuselage. After confirmation from another pilot, the Lufthansa pilot requests to leave the aircraft to close the door. After the pilot was cleared to close it, a little giggling from the Tower Controller ensues.
Listen to the audio.
http://bit.ly/9wmIDZ

NAUTICAL MILES
A knot is both an aviation and naval measurement; it is a mile per hour.

A nautical mile is one-sixtieth of a degree of longitude measured at the equator. The earth measures 21,600 nautical miles at the equator. That is 60 nautical miles to each degree for 360 degrees.

An English mile is 5,280 feet. A nautical mile is 6,082 feet or 1,852 meters.
http://en.wikipedia.org/wiki/Nautical_mile

LISTEN IN ON ATC AT JFK AIRPORT
This guy is always very happy on the job despite all the pressure and the stress.
http://bit.ly/hlT1m9

You think you have had a bad day at work. Once you have heard this think again. LOL.
http://bit.ly/h6bPok

☺ Humor

AIR TRAFFIC DANCER
Montage of a ground controller directing warplanes off to the friendly skies.
http://bit.ly/hDZEcW

TOWER TALK
Pilot: "Tower, request permission to enter your control zone."
Tower: "Negative."
Pilot: "Tower, did you say 'negative'?"
Tower: "Affirmative."
Pilot: "Understood 'affirmative'. Will call when leaving zone."

TOWER TALK
Pilot (KLM 242): "Good morning Zurich tower, KLM 242 requests start up and push back, please."
Tower: "KLM 242 Expect start up in two hours."
Pilot (KLM 242): "Please confirm: two hour delay??"
Tower: "Affirmative."
Pilot (KLM 242): "In that case, cancel the good morning!"

TOWER TALK
Tower: "Delta 351, you have traffic at 10 o'clock, 6 miles."
Delta 351: "Give us another hint! We have digital watches!"

TOWER TALK
Tower: "TWA 2341, for noise abatement turn right 45 degrees."
Pilot: "Center, we are at 35,000 feet. How much noise can we make up here?"
Tower: "Sir, have you ever heard the noise a 747 makes when it hits a 727?"

Chapter Seven
Airports

A. Airport Ratings & Statistics
B. Club Rooms
C. Boarding

A. Airport Ratings & Statistics

FACTOIDS

O'Hare Airport (ORD) was names for Butch O'Hare, a legendary WWII pilot.

O'Hare Airport was originally named "Orchard Field," ORD.

O'Hare Airport (ORD) employs more than 35,000 people.

Denver Airport (DEN/DIA) covers 53 sq miles/58 sq kms.

Los Angeles Airport (LAX) dumps some 8,000 tons of wasted food each year.

UK airports handled 218 million passengers during the 2009 calendar year.

Frankfurt Airport's winter timetable consists of 4,435 flight departures per week offered by 106 scheduled airlines flying to 266 destinations in 112 countries. This capacity corresponds to 680,000 seats per week. With 138 intercontinental destinations, more than half of Frankfurt Airport's destinations will be outside of Europe.

The world's highest commercial airport is La Paz, Bolivia (LPB) at 13,325 ft. / 4,061.5 m

Edwards Air Force Base (EDW) has the longest runway: 7.5-miles/11.5 km. It is the alternate landing site for the Space Shuttle.

Air travel employs some 28-million people worldwide.

THE AIRPORT OF THE FUTURE
Passengers will have more information and control. Airlines will reduce costs. Changes will be made to flight information, check-in, boarding, lost luggage and more. Technology can't solve all of the problems of air travel, but it can make the journey a little smoother.
http://aol.it/apECmJb

GREATEST CHALLENGE SAY AIRPORT EMPLOYEES ARE THE PASSENGERS

A family tried to sneak a dead man, propped up in a wheelchair, through airport security in New York. A couple had to be stopped while having sex in the corner of a Phoenix, Arizona, airport terminal. A man flying out of Chicago, Illinois, set a rat free, insisting he had to do this for religious purposes.

Many of those working in airports love what they do because they're touched and entertained by us.
http://bit.ly/h7lmjN

PEOPLE MOVERS-WALKWAYS

Those moving walkways are for saving you steps and to move passengers through the airport faster.

Some people have a lot of time between flights while others have short connections.

If you are not walking, stand to the right. That means your colleagues or family too.

Most walkways are narrow. Dulles (IAD) airport has conveniently wide walkways.

COMMERCIAL AVIATION NUMBERS

For the latest numbers on air and other travel see the Bureau of Transportation Statistics pages.
http://www.bts.gov/

AIRPORT USER RATINGS

Read what others say about the facilities before you pass though them. See
http://bit.ly/cZUh9v
http://www.worldtravelguide.net/airports

FIND 9,485 AIRPORT CODES AROUND THE WORLD
Abbreviations, runway lengths, and other airport information. See
http://www.world-airport-codes.com/
http://bit.ly/a6uEBg
http://bit.ly/eCMP1D
http://www.airlinecodes.co.uk/home.asp

THE WORLD'S BUSIEST AIRPORTS
Atlanta: 8.4 million passengers in July 2010.
Beijing Capital: 6.8 million.
London/Heathrow: 6.7 million.
Chicago/O'Hare: 6.4 million.
Paris/CDG: 5.8 million.

AIRPORT CHARGES PER PASSENGER
The cost per enplaned passenger, the typical measure of airport costs for an airline, is about $14.50 at Ontario, California (ONT), more than double the U.S. median.

In comparison with other Southern California airports, Burbank's (BUR) cost per passenger is $2.10, John Wayne's (SNA) is $9.93 and Los Angeles (LAX) is $11.
http://bit.ly/bNnz3U

MOST EXPENSIVE AIRPORTS
Which airports have the highest airfares? Huntsville, Alabama, is the highest and Long Beach, California, is the lowest.
See the Peter Greenberg video.
http://bit.ly/hspIdB

FLYING/AIRLINE ACRONYMS
TPAC, SWU, BIS, DBC, MLL. No we are not swearing. These are airline codes flyers should know. For a glossary and lists of these acronyms, see http://flyertalk.com/glossary/
and
http://bit.ly/aOlWAi

LANDINGS: THE BUSIEST AVIATION WEBSITE IN CYBERSPACE
Lots of aviation news
http://www.landings.com/

TAKEOFF AND LANDING DISTANCES
Sometimes it seems as though the plane is rolling a long way before takeoff. Takeoff distance is affected by the loaded weight of the plane, air temperature, condition of the runway, elevation of the airport, etc.

If the runway is wet, the plane must overcome the additional friction.
At higher temperatures, the air is thinner and more roll is required to achieve liftoff speed.

Landing: If the runway is wet, more distance is required to avoid slipping/skidding, just as with an automobile.

TOUGH AIRPORTS
These U.S. airports have short runways. Landings are not likely to be slow and smooth.

Midway (MDW), Jackson Hole (JAC), John Wayne (SNA), and Reagan National (DCA).

MOST EXTREME AIRPORTS CROSSWIND LANDING HONG KONG'S (OLD) KAI TAK AIRPORT

Filmed from the checkerboard used for the approach into Kai Tak. The plane overshoots and then lines it up just to get caught in the wind...again. Unedited. You can hear another enthusiast in the background with a scanner. A Japan Air Lines JAL Boeing 747.
http://bit.ly/gXwkfZ

GATE 13

Many airports do not have a gate 13 to prevent passengers from worrying. Try to find gate 13 when you visit each airport.
Many hotels do not have a 13th floor.

NEED DIRECTIONS AT THE AIRPORT?

Don't ask a pilot (in uniform). They visit so many airports that they usually do not know.

NEW YORK AIRPORT TRAFFIC

--Joe Brancatelli, USA.

New York holds a crucial spot for business travelers. And among airlines operating from the region's airports, it's no surprise that the competition is ferocious, the expenditures extravagant, and the infighting brutal.

An estimated 130 million travelers annually use the region's three major airports (John F. Kennedy, LaGuardia, and Newark) as well as three secondary aerodromes (Islip on Long Island, Westchester

County, and Stewart Airport in New York's Hudson Valley).

New York generates $8 billion annually just in domestic revenue from airlines. A third of all transatlantic traffic flows through New York; four times more than the next largest U.S. market. Eighty international airlines serve the area. The world's most important international route, New York-London, is part of the mix. New York is also on one end of eight of the 10 busiest domestic routes. And airline insiders say New York-Los Angeles, the nation's busiest domestic route with more than 4,000 passengers a day, accounts for more revenue than some smaller airline hubs.
Read more: http://bit.ly/dzfAqd

AIRLINE GAME: VIRTUAL PILOT
Find the airport.
See http://bit.ly/cRfkSu

AIR TRAVEL IN THE PHILIPPINES
Because it consists of more than 7,000 islands, the most efficient way to travel in the Southeast Asian nation of the Philippines is to take an airplane.

The Philippines feature ten international airports and more than 200 domestic airports
http://bit.ly/b6EBVs

WHY YOU SHOULD ARRIVE AT THE AIRPORT AT LEAST TWO HOURS BEFORE YOUR FLIGHT
--Dan Poynter, USA.

Overnight snow, traffic jams, extra security checks, etc.

All have happened to me. Plan to arrive at the airport at least two hours before your flight.

CHECK-IN LINES
You are flying Coach and the Economy line at the check-in counter reaches to the next state. Fortunately, you are dressed nicely and the premium lines are down to zero.

Be nice; ask if the counter-person can serve you. They usually will if you are not bumping a high-paying customer.

Airlines want the Business and First Class lines to look sharp in case a high-paying customer shows up. And they do not want backpackers jumping into the shorter lines. Do not try this if you have brightly dyed hair, facial piercings, bare feet, or are wearing T-shirts & jeans.

AIRPORT ACTIVITIES
Peter Greenberg describes surprising finds in global airports like gyms, pet areas, kid play areas, dental facilities, casinos, hotels, and spas.
http://bit.ly/eTnCnI
http://bit.ly/gMX6R9

FASTER DEPARTING AND ARRIVING
In the early morning, depart from Arrivals. No one is arriving at the airport early. Do the opposite when being picked up late in the evening.
Peter Greenberg video.
http://bit.ly/h4Lr7M

B. Club Rooms

MOST AIRLINES HAVE CLUB ROOMS
There is usually an annual charge but you can often pay with miles and once you reach a certain number of miles, say 2 million, membership is free. Rooms often have free food, coffee, tea, etc. and a nice place to plug in your computer to work.

In addition to such Red Carpet Clubs, there are often clubs for Business Class and for International First Class. These are smaller, have better food and drink, and are more exclusive.

C. Boarding

Board earliest in your category to get an overhead bin for your bag near your seat.

FACTOID
Passengers always board the left side of an airliner, just as they board the "port" side of a ship.

☺ Humor
DAFFYNITIONS
--Joe Heuer, http://daffynitions.com, USA.

Airport: The place you take your spouse when he or she wants to go out for a really expensive meal.

TIM HAWKINS ON THE BOARDING ANNOUNCEMENT
http://bit.ly/i6EebX

Chapter Eight
Country Information

A. Travel Statistics & Advice by Country
   Embassies
B. People/Leaders
C. Canada
D. U.S.

A. Travel Statistics & Advice by Country

SPECIFIC COUNTRY IFORMATION
Get information on every country in the world. For each country, you will find information such as the location of the U.S. embassy and any consular offices; whether you need a visa; crime and security information; health and medical conditions; drug penalties; and localized hot spots.

This is a good place to start learning about where you plan to go.
http://bit.ly/gZENEG
http://bit.ly/cJMNmz
Capsulations from the United Nations. See
http://bit.ly/bmY9yp

THE WORLD FACTBOOK
The World Factbook remains the CIA's most widely disseminated and most popular product; millions of visitors frequent the online *Factbook* each month. In

addition, tens of thousands of government, commercial, academic, and other Web sites link to, or replicate, the online version of the *Factbook*.

This reference site is updated biweekly throughout the year to provide wide-ranging and hard-to-locate information about the background, geography, people, government, economy, communications, transportation, military, and transnational issues for countries from Afghanistan to Zimbabwe. Included among the 271 geographic entries is one for the "World," which incorporates data and other information summarized where possible from the other 270 country listings.
http://bit.ly/gzh2tf

THE ECONOMIST and BBC COUNTRY PROFILES
Before you leave, read about the economic outlook, politics, basic facts, history, etc. See
http://bit.ly/daQqGC

CONSULAR INFORMATION SHEETS
The latest information about a country published by the United States, Australia, United Kingdom, Canada, and New Zealand. See
http://bit.ly/abdPOD

INTERNATIONAL NUMBER ONE
Because each country is the best at something. See the chart at
http://bit.ly/bAgFUL

EMBASSYWORLD
A directory & search engine of the world's Embassies & Consulates.
http://bit.ly/cmdnY7

WEB SITES OF FOREIGN EMBASSIES IN THE U.S.
See
http://bit.ly/axLhLt

B. People/Leaders

WHO'S IN CHARGE?
This site provides detailed chronologies, flags, national anthems, maps and indexes to enhance your research into the world of history and politics. It is a complete and up-to-date encyclopedia of the leaders of nations and territories. International organizations and recent religious leaders are listed separately. See
http://bit.ly/autu5o

WORLD LEADERS
The CIA publishes and updates this online directory of *Chiefs of State and Cabinet Members of Foreign Governments* regularly. The directory is intended to be used primarily as a reference aid and includes as many governments of the world as is considered practical, some of them not officially recognized by the United States.

Governments are listed in alphabetical order according to the most commonly used version of each country's name. The spelling of the personal names

in this directory follows transliteration systems generally agreed upon by US Government agencies, except in the cases in which officials have stated a preference for alternate spellings of their names.
http://bit.ly/gzh2tf

FORMS OF ADDRESS
How to address a letter or a person. See
http://bit.ly/doSdg3

C. Canada

INFORMATION FOR CANADIAN CITIZENS REGARDING WESTERN HEMISPHERE TRAVEL INITIATIVE (WHTI) AND AIR TRAVEL
Canadian citizens traveling by air to, through, or from the United States must present a valid passport or a valid NEXUS card when used at kiosks at participating airports. This requirement applies to all travelers, regardless of age, including children.
http://www.cbsa-asfc.gc.ca

CANADA BUSINESS
Includes links to business travel to Canada, doing business in Canada, embassies & consulates, currency converters, maps, etc. A Canadian Government site. See
http://bit.ly/9qpQl8

BUSINESS IN CANADA
Get business and consumer information and statistics from Industry Canada. There are links to company directories, business information by sector,

licenses, legislation, copyright information, etc. A
Canadian Government site. See
http://bit.ly/aKjJEq

D. United States

**READ WHAT THE INTERNATIONAL PRESS IS
SAYING ABOUT THE U.S.**
--Pat Tith, USA.

http://bit.ly/8XvQfG

Chapter Nine
Trip Planning

A. Places to Visit
B. Visas & Vaccination Requirments
C. Passports
D. Clothing
E. Dining: Eating & Food

A. Places to Visit

TRAVEL RESOURCE
--Beverly Babb, CAE, USA.

The IATA Travel Centre provides personalized advice for travel planning and trip preparation. Passport, Visa and Health requirements, as well as customs, airport tax, and currency information are a simple click away.
http://bit.ly/bsSgSq

✈ **FLYERTALK**
Flyertalk, part of the WebFlyer Network, features discussions and chat boards that cover the most up-to-date traveler information. Just choose a forum and you can get to the business at hand: conversing about programs, how to make the most of your miles and points, general travel, airports, destination and dining information. See
http://bit.ly/98yqv4

TRAVELER PERSONALITY QUIZ

You and your spouse may take this quiz. Find out what type of traveler your significant other is. Then when you plan for a trip to a distant venue, check whether it matches your spouse's profile. If so, take him or her along for the trip.

For the Travel Personality Quiz, see
http://bit.ly/bGo9Dr , http://bit.ly/a9DvbI

TRAVEL TIPS

Visas, safety, advice, etc. from the U.S. Department of State. See
http://www.travel.state.gov/
http://bit.ly/gKPorX

SURVEY ON INTERNATIONAL TOURISTS REVEALS

--Italians are best dressed
--Japanese are the most polite
--Americans try the hardest to speak local languages and are the best tippers

The survey was carried out among employees in 4,000 hotels in Germany, the U.K., Italy, France, Canada, and the U.S.

Respondents were asked to rank clients by nationality on criteria of general attitude, politeness, tendency to complain, willingness to speak local languages, interest in sampling local cuisine, readiness to spend money, generosity, cleanliness, discretion and elegance.
http://bit.ly/aBC6Ui

HOW TO MAKE A GOOD IMPRESSION IN ASIA
Business cards, what to wear, meal etiquette and more.
http://bit.ly/dAEBWF

ALL-INCLUSIVE RESORTS
A video with Peter Greenberg.
http://bit.ly/hdYNDw

BOOKING BUDDY is a free service designed to help travelers search all their favorite travel websites with fewer clicks and in less time. It is a service of *Smarter Living, Inc.* See
http://bit.ly/aTWmIy

U.S. VISITOR INFORMATION
History, doing business and working in the States. See
http://bit.ly/alLLF2

TRAVEL-WATCH
Travel-Watch is a news service with some 40 news, features, and reviews daily (Monday through Friday) for approximately 124,000 subscribers. Subscribers include frequent travelers, corporate travel managers, travel agents, and other publications. Approximately 385, newspapers, magazines, TV, and Radio stations carry Travel Watch's stories.
http://www.travel-watch.com/

TRAVEL REVIEWS YOU CAN TRUST
Get recommendations from other travelers. See the real people behind the advice. Share your own reviews and photos to earn rewards.
http://www.igougo.com/

WORLD STATISTICS
See the numbers change as you watch.
http://bit.ly/bVh912

TRAVEL TIPS FROM MILLION MILERS
Audio interviews. MP3 downloads. See
http://www.themillionmileclub.com/

"A good traveler has no fixed plans and is not intent on arriving."
--Lao Tzu, sixth century, BCE. Chinese Taoist philosopher.

BUSINESS CARDS
Many people are opting for slick or "coated" stock when ordering new business cards. Cards that are shiny on one surface allow you to put your photograph on one side and your contact information on the other.

Now many printers offer card stock that is C2S or Coated 2 Sides. While cards printed on C2S stock look and feel nice, recipients can't write reminder notes on them.

Suggestions: Order cards on C1S stock and carry small Post-it® notes for sticking to the C2S cards that are given to you.

IS YOUR BUSINESS CARD WORKING FOR YOU?
http://bit.ly/8ZfnRQ

EXCHANGING BUSINESS CARDS IN ASIA
Across Asia, business success depends heavily on contacts liking and trusting you. By showing correct etiquette, you will help them feel at ease. But knowing the customs and what is considered polite or not can be difficult in this vast, culturally diverse region.

The exchange of business cards is serious business. Customs vary between countries, so to avoid offense:

Always accept a card with both hands – this is universally regarded as good manners.

Examine it for a few moments and then place it in front of you during the meeting.

Never hastily stuff it into your pocket or bag.

Don't write on another person's card.

Remember to hand out your cards to everybody in a meeting.

For more tips, see
http://bit.ly/dAEBWF

TRAVEL PLANNING INFORMATION
See Travel Tools at iTravelnet
http://bit.ly/cRNq0N

WIKITRAVEL
Wikitravel is a project to create a free, complete, up-to-date, and reliable worldwide travel guide. So far they have 21,611 destination guides and other articles written and edited by Wikitravellers from around the globe.
http://bit.ly/98T7sQ

USEFUL LINKS FOR YOUR INTERNATIONAL TRIP
--Elisabeth Heller, © Heller Consult,
www.hellerconsult.com

Country Information
The CIA World Fact Book http://bit.ly/dBC30O
The World Trade Organization http://www.wto.org
Reporters without Borders http://www.rsf.org
World Travel Guide http://www.worldtravelguide.net
International Chamber of Commerce
http://bit.ly/djr2QT
Nations Encyclopedia
http://www.nationsencyclopedia.com

Languages
Multi-Language Dictionary http://dict.leo.org
Foreign Language Online Dictionaries
http://bit.ly/czOUia

Business Behavior
International Business Behavior
http://www.cyborlink.com
Geert Hofstede's Personal Website
http://stuwww.uvt.nl/~csmeets/PAGE3.HTM

Religion
Wikipedia on the major religious groups around the world.
http://bit.ly/bh1Fij

ASIA-PACIFIC RESOURCES FOR TRAVELERS
Airlines, hotels, bargain travel sites and more.
--Mike Podolinsky, Singapore.
http://bit.ly/c2s7Zn

PLACE TO VISIT WITH CHILDREN, BY COUNTRY
http://www.travelforkids.com/

ONLINE TRAVEL RESOURCE JUST FOR WOMEN
http://www.journeywoman.com/

TIPS FOR TRAVELING AND BUSINESS IN THE UAE
From Ali Al Saloom's web site. *Just Ask Ali.*
http://www.ask-ali.com/a2ztravelguide.asp#A

USA TODAY FLIGHT INFO SITE
http://usat.ly/hzgKh7

CULTURES APP
The iPhone/iPad App *Cultures* covers greetings, communication style, personal space, touching, eye contact, views of time, gender issues, gestures, phrases, etc.
See the Apple App Store.

AIRLINE AMBASSADORS
Peter Greenberg on how you can help people in other countries.
http://bit.ly/fRWRjk

VOLUNTEER VACATIONS
Peter Greenberg talks about a completely fulfilling type of vacation. Volunteer vacations from wild horse farms to Habitat for Humanity.
http://bit.ly/ejAUij

PLACES NOT TO VISIT
"The city of five smells" and more. Video with Peter Greenberg.
http://bit.ly/fAr20o

B. Visas & Vaccination Requirments
Also see the chapter on Health.

VISA & SHOT REQUIREMENTS BY COUNTRY
Get specific information on travel documents and health requirements for the area(s) you will be visiting. See
http://bit.ly/bVyIO0

CENTER FOR DISEASE CONTROL AND PREVENTION
The CDC has links for travelers regarding necessary vaccinations, health information for specific destinations, and information for international travelers with disabilities, among others.

The CDC is one of the 13 major operating components of the Department of Health and Human

Services (HHS), which is the principal agency in the United States government for protecting health and safety. See
http://www.cdc.gov/travel/

C. Passports

STEPS TO FOLLOW WHEN APPLYING FOR A NEW U. S. PASSPORT
There are seven steps that you must take during the application process; here are a few tips that can help you along the way.
http://bit.ly/hzN2pG
http://bit.ly/hX56G7
http://www.uspassportnow.com/services
Video
http://bit.ly/fsLZqq

THE U.S. STATE DEPARTMENT ISSUED A RECORD 18.4 MILLION PASSPORTS IN FISCAL YEAR 2007, COMPARED TO 12.1 MILLION IN 2006.
The increase was due to new laws requiring passports for all North American and Caribbean countries. Previously, U.S. citizens needed only a form of identification such as a driver's license. See
http://bit.ly/dCZriO

LOST YOUR PASSPORT—WHAT NEXT?
You will need to get special documentation from your embassy or consulate. And you may miss your flight.
http://bit.ly/9COfrJ

NEW RULES ON VISA-FREE ENTRY INTO THE USA

The legal requirements for entering the United States changed on 12 January 2009. Online registration is required before departure.

Passengers, who do not permanently reside in the U.S. and who are entering the USA without a visa as part of the "Visa Waiver Program" must register online before departure with the "Electronic System for Travel Authorization", or "ESTA". As authorization can take up to 72 hours, passengers should register as early as possible. Children also require their own, separate ESTA registration.

ESTA registration is available free to travelers at https://esta.cbp.dhs.gov. The information required is explained in form I-94W. The online ESTA system guides travelers in various languages, including English. All answers are to be given in English.

The entered information is transmitted online to the relevant U.S. authorities and a personal registration number is allocated. Registered customers will received a confirmation email with notification of the approval or rejection of their entry application.

Should the destination address or any other travel details change after approval, then this information can be updated online on the ESTA website at any time using the registration number.

Registration is not required for passengers entering the USA with a visa, American or Canadian nationals, or passengers with a Resident Green Card for the USA.

Registration may be done by the individual or by a third party, e.g. family member. For other visits to the USA within the validity period of two years--provided the holder's passport is still valid--the information only has to be updated online.

In addition to the ESTA registration, the airline transporting the passenger is still required to record personal details for entry into the USA.

The procedure is similar to U.S. citizens traveling to Australia.

VISA & PASSPORT INFORMATION
http://bit.ly/9x1I2R

ADDING PAGES TO A U.S. PASSPORT
Passport nearly full? If you have a few years left before the expiration date, there is no need to apply for a new passport. The Department of State will add 24 more pages. Apparently there is a charge now; the extra pages used to be free. And, the upgrade often takes less than two weeks.

Get Form DS-4085: Application for Additional Visa Pages at http://bit.ly/a6iHzD
Peter Greenberg video on passport tips.
http://bit.ly/gpolUC

D. Clothing

IMAGE MAKEOVER BEFORE AND AFTER
--Sandy Dumont, USA.

The way you look and dress telegraphs the outcome other people can expect from you. It also announces how you feel about yourself, and you'll be treated accordingly. You must look "state-of-the-art" from head to toe. If even one element of your image looks out of sync or dated, you will be judged as also having dated messages, products, or skills.

Don't play Wardrobe Roulette™ with your image!
See the before and after photos at
http://bit.ly/ab6xiD

E. Dining: Eating and Food

SAVE 15% ON RESTAURANT MEETINGS IN SINGAPORE
If you host a large meeting with a meal (breakfast, lunch, high tea or dinner) at a hotel such as the Royal Plaza on Scotts (recommended by Scott Friedman), they will cut 15% from the bill if you pay with certain credit cards. The cards must be UOB, DBS, Citibank or AMEX; apparently, in Singapore, hotels and banks promote business this way.

The discount is for food only and ended on 31 December 2009. Ask if it has been renewed. You must notify the F&B manager in advance; request their price chart. A party of ten can save nearly S$100.

☺ **Humor**

DAFFYNITIONS
--Joe Heuer, http://daffynitions.com, USA.

Travel: what you are definitely too sick to do if you actually look like your passport photo.

WHEN YOUR FACE DOES NOT MATCH YOUR PASSPORT PHOTO
Humorous video on Passport Control.
http://bit.ly/ezyGKQ

Chapter Ten
Borders

A. Customs
B. Immigration

On arrival, read the signs. Do not follow other people. Some may be lost, some may be connecting to other flights, and some may be heading to the local-citizens' lines. Most airports have separate lines for local passport holders.

A. Customs

DECLARE ANYTHING YOU ARE NOT SURE ABOUT
Canada prohibits fruit but bananas are OK (Canada is not protecting a banana crop.) Australia lets in protein bars if you declare them. If you do not declare questionable items and are caught, you can be charged with "lying on an official document." You will be subject to severe fines and jail time.
When in doubt, declare.

WORKING IN CANADA AND TAXES
--Ian Percy, ian@ianpercy.com, Canada.

If you pay your income tax in the US and you want to work in Canada you have two choices.

If your fees are not predetermined (e.g. you are holding a public seminar and you don't know what revenue will be generated) then pay the Canadian tax and reclaim it when you prepare your U.S. taxes.

You pay taxes in one country and you indicate that you've paid it in the U.S., Canada will refund the money usually within 2-3 months. Your accountant should know how to do this. I believe the form used is found here: http://bit.ly/dJxOc0
but check with your accountant.

If your fees are set and you know exactly what you're being paid then fill in Waiver Form 105 found at http://bit.ly/hjFuR2
and send it in to the appropriate Revenue Canada office *well ahead of your actual engagement date.* You will get back a waiver and your client or bureau will not need to withhold the 15% tax. No need to do anything with the waiver other than let your client know you have it. They may want a copy but usually I just keep it in that client's file.

All this applies to fees for service only and not expenses. In Canada you will pay a "GST" tax on all purchases much of which you can also get back if you keep all receipts. You can find the forms at the airport. Unless you've been there for a substantial amount of time, however, it's not worth doing.

There is a Tax Information Phone Service (TIPS) hotline at 1-800-267-6999 that is quite helpful.

Actually there is a third option. You can take the risk that your client is clueless about all of this and they'll just pay your invoice. Frankly that is a good way to be black listed at the border so is not recommended. And please no whining--it is just as much a nuisance going from Canada to the US. There is a huge part of "Free Trade" that is purely mythical.

Usual disclaimers: I'm not an accountant and all are advised to check with an international tax professional.

B. Immigration

THE FASTER IMMIGRATION LINE
--Michael Podolinsky

Move to the line (queue) next to the special row for flight crew; usually to the left. When flight crew is not going through immigration, many times the officer will wave in the next person from the closest line. Often much faster.

THE IMMIGRATION SHORT LINE
If you travel often internationally, you may sign up for special programs. Machines providing iris scans or finger print checks are available in the

U.S., Canada, The Netherlands, Singapore and some other countries. http://on.wsj.com/bxVqEk

US: **Global Entry** machines were in 20 international airports at the beginning of 2011.
http://bit.ly/djdYnI
https://goes-app.cbp.dhs.gov/
http://cbp.gov/

US/Canada: **NEXUS**
http://bit.ly/djdYnI
The NEXUS card is good for five years. Put your application date on the back or the storage envelope. Do not expect to be notified of renewal time. See http://bit.ly/aGOFcA

If the system is down or if you have some items to declare, when going through immigration, you are in the short line and will still zip on through.

Always fill out a landing card/declaration form in case the machine is not working or the system is down. Then you can whip out your form, have it stamped, and proceed without delay.

NEXUS/FAST CARDS UPDATE
Passports not required.

Citizens of the United States and Canada may now use their NEXUS and Free And Secure Trade (FAST) cards as proof of identification and citizenship at all land border lanes and seaport locations (not just the NEXUS/FAST lanes) when entering the United States or Canada.
http://www.cbp.gov/

IMMIGRATION LINE: IAD IS SAID TO BE THE FRIENDLIEST U.S. AIRPORT

Some frequent international flyers prefer landing at Dulles International Airport near Washington, DC.

They say the immigration and customs officers are super polite because they do not know which passengers are well-connected. They could be Congressional staffers or other government officials.

JOAN RIVERS DENIED BOARDING IN PUERTO RICO

Her passport had the name "Joan Rosenberg, AKA Joan Rivers." It did not match the name on the ticket.

Hear Larry King interview her on CNN. http://bit.ly/gUZPf1

☺ **Humor**

HOW TO CLEAR CUSTOMS

With all the recent customs fee hikes and unnecessary increased security (another fee there), what's a cuzzy to do?
Billy T. James gives us some tips with this classic clip. http://bit.ly/fjqbxM

Chapter Eleven
Events Around the World

A. Calendars of Events.
B. Video Conferencing vs. Being There
C. Specific Countries

A. **Calendars of Events.**
Find events to attend in your travels and connections for business opportunities. Make all or part of your trip tax deductible.

WHATSonWHEN
Plan your journey around festivals, performances, even meteor showers in locations around the globe. This site lets you plan travel based on your interests, and makes sure you don't miss an important event.

You can search by location and/or date. Just a few of the event topics are: Adventure, Classical Music, Clubs & Parties, Film, Food & Drink, Heritage, Jazz, Kids & Family, Literature, Music, Natural Phenomena, Opera, Performing & Visual Arts.
http://bit.ly/btybIs

MICE CALENDAR
See events all over the world on the MICE (Meetings, Incentives, Conferences, and Exhibitions) calendar. http://bit.ly/bQrJSn

WORLDWIDE TRADE SHOW DIRECTORY.
See if there are trade shows you might visit on your next trip. If you find a match with your line of work, the trip may be tax deductable. Listed are 7,201 trade shows, exhibitions, and conferences coming from 1,585 fairs organizers, with a total of 12,839 events. See http://bit.ly/cywOR0

RESOURCES FOR GOING GLOBAL
The Commerce Department's mission is to help make U.S. businesses more innovative at home and more competitive abroad. The U.S. Commercial Service has offices across the United States and in more than 75 countries. The USCS uses its global Network and international resources to connect U.S companies with international buyers worldwide. To find the trade specialist nearest you, visit http://www.buyusa.gov/home/us.html

B. Video Conferencing vs. Being There

MORE VIDEO CONFERENCING—LESS AIR TRAVEL
Experts have predicted it and now the research confirms that IT decision makers will continue to buy video conferencing technology, as companies target travel budgets as money gets tight. http://bit.ly/axwFfy

FACE-TO-FACE MEETINGS STILL IMPORTANT
In an Orbitz survey, 92% of respondents said in-person meetings are important to their work productivity. http://bit.ly/9cWfYx

SEEING IS BELIEVING
Why face-to-face meetings are important.
--Michael Podolinsky, Singapore.

The Singapore Air Show has already returned $14-Billion in Deals! And it's not over. Why?

In the video, I show you a small shot of the Singapore Air Show and share a reason WHY they do it and then apply it to our lives. Visibility and seeing the REAL THING IN ACTION is much more effective than just reading about it or looking at a picture.

Movies are good but the impact of the heat from thrusters, the smell of the jet fuel, the DRAMA of contrails, and the speed, make air shows (and our lives) so much more exciting. http://bit.ly/9fmG91

C. Specific Countries

SHANGHAI IS TRYING TO UNTANGLE THE MANGLED ENGLISH OF CHINGLISH

For the past two years, the Shanghai Commission for the Management of Language Use has been trying to clean up English-language signs and menus to rid them of their malapropisms.

For English speakers with subpar Chinese skills, daily life in China offers a confounding array of choices. At banks, there are machines for "cash withdrawing" and "cash recycling." The menus of local restaurants might present such delectables as "fried enema," "monolithic tree mushroom stem squid" and a mysterious thirst-quencher known as "The Jew's Ear Juice."

Article:
http://nyti.ms/99TlTw

Comment:
http://nyti.ms/9UJeCR

☺ **Humor**

MIKE PODOLINSKY DOES STANDUP EXPLAINING SINGAPORE
See
http://bit.ly/c7bElV

Chapter Twelve
Money, Credit Cards, Exchange Rates, Fees, & Taxes

A. Money
B. Credit Cards
C. Exchange Rates
D. Fees and Taxes
E. Tipping
F. Airline Frequent Flyer & Hotel Frequent Stay Programs
G. Airfares
H. Air Travel Insurance.

A. Money

GET MONEY BACK WHEN AIRFARES DROP
If you buy an airline ticket only to see the price fall, there is something you can do about it.

Many airlines will give refunds if they cut the price after you have bought a ticket. Alaska, JetBlue, Southwest, United and US Airways all offer vouchers for the full price difference. For example, if the price drops $200, you can get a $200 coupon towards a future trip. Other air carriers offer vouchers, or cash, after deducting change fees (which can run up to $100). Ask.
See
http://yhoo.it/aGjbcI

FINDING ATMs/CASH MACHINES WITH YOUR iPHONE

Automatic Teller Machines are a place to get local currency and travelers say they offer the best currency exchange rates.

See the App Store for *ATM Hunter*. The iPhone uses GPS to find your location and then *ATM Hunter* lists the nearest machine by address and distance. It works worldwide.

In the UK, ATMs are called "Cash Machines."

TAKING CASH OUT OF A COUNTRY
-- Marcia Reynolds, CSP, http://www.OutsmartYourBrain.com, USA.

This may not be a surprise to many, but when leaving a country, check if they have restrictions on how much cash you can carry when you leave. It has been many years since anyone has asked me this, so I wasn't even thinking about it when I was asked how much cash I had by Customs in Ukraine. My client paid the balance of my fee in cash, U.S. dollars, as many of my Eastern European clients do since they don't seem to trust their banks. Customs took $1500 of the $4500 I was carrying, telling me I should have known that they had a $3000 limit. My client was aghast, telling me she thought it was $10,000. Who knows? It might be corruption. All I know is that it was a tough lesson for me to learn.

B. Credit Cards

AIRLINE CREDIT CARDS COMPARED

After miles for airline flights, the next-most-important source of miles for most frequent flyers is the credit card itself. And for good reason. Cards with a mileage-earning component give users a way to "double dip" (earn miles for the flight, the hotel or the car rental as well as earn miles for credit card purchases which would not otherwise fall under the mileage umbrella.) See http://bit.ly/b4Tv8Y

There are some good value cards out there but you must choose carefully and for those who can't pay their balances in full each month, you're better off going for a credit card with a low interest rate. The rewards may be smaller but you'll save money in the long run, http://bit.ly/gY9LU8

See the card comparison chart.
http://bit.ly/dwES6h

AIRLINE CREDIT CARDS
Why the airlines love them.
http://bit.ly/apcvg4

CREDIT CARDS THAT OFFER MILES
The only cards that earn miles in airline accounts are the cards co-branded with the airline—and each major airline co-brands one credit card—plus the American Express and Diners Club cards that allow you to transfer card credit into miles in participating airline programs. http://bit.ly/ctEHZQ, http://bit.ly/95SeV1

WHAT HAPPENS WHEN YOUR CREDIT CARD NUMBERS ARE STOLEN

Federal prosecutors revealed indictments against 38 people, accusing them of running a national airline-ticket fraud that involved buying tickets using stolen identities and selling the tickets at a steep discount-- usually $100 or $200.

At least two of the people accused of stealing credit card and debit card information obtained it from hotels where they worked.
http://bit.ly/94liiy

BEWARE OVERSEAS CREDIT CARD FEES
--Kristin Arnold, USA.

Many banks are charging exorbitant fees when travelers use their credit cards outside their countries. You can get hit with these surcharges if you withdraw cash from foreign ATMs or even when you pay for your hotel stay.

Be aware that if you charge a ticket with a foreign airline or cruise line, your bank may tack on a 1% or more "Foreign Transaction Fee."

BTW, the Kristin Arnold referenced in the article is not the professional speaker Kristin Arnold but she did send in this news item.
http://bit.ly/chdF98

CREDIT CARD FEES ON OVERSEAS CHARGES
Some add 1-3%.

A Peter Greenberg video.
http://bit.ly/hspIdB

PRIORITY CLUB VISA ELIMINATES INTERNATIONAL TRANSACTION FEES
Priority Club card (Crowne Plaza, Holiday Inn, Intercontinental, etc.) does not charge fees on products and services you purchase in other countries.
http://bit.ly/acEyLY

✈ FLYERTALK FORUM ON CREDIT CARD PROGRAMS/PARTNERS
http://www.flyertalk.com/forum/miles-points-1/

NOTIFY YOUR CREDIT CARD COMPANY OF PLANNED TRAVEL OUTSIDE YOUR OWN COUNTRY
--Norman Zalfa, past Director of Security, ITT Europe.

Most credit card company's security programs will automatically reject a payment when the computer sees an unusual charge in an area not normally used by the cardholder.

Carry more than one credit card.

VISA AND MASTERCARD INTERNATIONAL CHALLENGES
Carry some local cash. Your card may not be accepted everywhere.

U.S. cards continue to rely on old-fashioned magnetic stripes while European cards (and point-of-sale terminals) are moving to chip-based systems. See http://bit.ly/9x0oBH

CREDIT CARDS WITH RFID CHIPS
A number of credit card companies now issue credit cards with embedded RFIDs (radio frequency ID tags), with promises of enhanced security and speedy transactions. But on today's episode of Boing Boing TV, hacker and inventor Pablos Holman shows Xeni how you can use about $8 worth of gear bought on eBay to read personal data from those credit cards: cardholder name, credit card number, and whatever else your bank embeds in this manner. See http://www.youtube.com/watch?v=vmajlKJlT3U http://www.idstronghold.com/

SOME INTERNATIONAL MERCHANTS REQUEST A PIN
If a store asks for a PIN, tell the clerk this is a credit card not a debit card. They usually accept it. As a backup, carry a debit card.

USE YOUR CREDIT CARD TO GET THE PRICE DOWN
Offer to pay with a credit card; then the merchant will agree to a lower price for cash so he can avoid the credit-card fees.
A Peter Greenberg video tip. http://bit.ly/g0owa7

C. Exchange Rates

BEST EXCHANGE RATES
Many travelers find the best rates to be from ATMs, called "Cash Machines" in the UK or a bank. Bureaux de Change and hotels charge more to change your money. If you want to change money from the last country you visited to the next one, the bureaux de change may charge you twice: from your last country to local currency and then again for your next country.

CURRENCY CONVERSION PROGRAM FOR iPHONE

iPhone App: *Units* converts energy, temperature, area, time, length, weight, speed, pressure, power, currency, volume and data storage.
Free. See the Apple App Store.

iPhone App: *Currency*
Check conversion rates for more than 90 currencies worldwide with *Currency*. Choose your master currency, enter an amount, and see what that purchase would cost back home. Free.
See the Apple App Store.

INTERNATIONAL CURRENCY CONVERSION
See and bookmark this site: http://bit.ly/bbZXhI

CURRENCY CONVERSIONS
FXCheatSheet allows travelers to create and print a currency converter table for their next trip. To get a copy of your currency table, select the language,

date, currencies you wish to obtain and the rate you believe is most relevant to your needs. Click on "Get my FXCheatSheet" to get a copy of your FXCheatSheet. See http://bit.ly/9BGhT0

D. Fees and Taxes

IATA LISTS TAXES AND FEES FOR PASSENGERS

They are: airport taxes, paid to a "collecting authority", for international and domestic departures, and arrivals taxes; passenger charges for facilities and services at airports; stamp taxes - for stamps affixed to tickets; and ticket taxes, which are included in the ticket price and levied at the time of sale.

HOW MUCH DO AIRLINES MAKE ON BAG FEES?

Baggage fees account for between $350 and 400 million dollars USD a year for United Airlines. http://bit.ly/dqzAYD

AIRLINES ADD FEES, AND SOME FEES ON TOP OF FEES

For example, Spanish airline Vueling charges a fee to pick a seat. Any seat at all. A "basic" seat behind the wing runs 3 euros. For 30 euros, travelers can choose an aisle or window seat and guarantee that the middle seat will remain empty.

The following are fees charged to most coach passengers. Very frequent fliers and passengers with full-fare tickets may be exempt from some fees. http://bit.ly/atVKud, http://bit.ly/9xu83y

TEN "SNEAKY" AIRLINE FEES
--Beverly Babb, USA.

Carriers don't want to raise ticket prices, so they're looking for new ways to reach into travelers' wallets, charging extra for seat selection, phone reservations, and even pillows.
http://on.msn.com/9GgACk

AVOIDING AIRLINE FEES
Peter Greenberg describes new fees added on by airlines and gives tips on how to avoid them.
http://bit.ly/iexdxl

UNITED AIRLINES DIVULGES ON-TIME SECRETS
And a way to avoid bag-check fees

United station managers tackle problems as soon as they occur. They try to have people discuss the problem right then and there—without blame.

United starts boarding 30 minutes before departure—not 27 minutes or 28 minutes. On flights with a high share of business fliers, who tend to avoid checking bags, United asks for volunteers to plane-check bags. Then, when it begins boarding passengers with lower boarding priority, it insists on checked bags.

United does not charge to check bags planeside, because timeliness, rather than revenue, takes priority.

Those holding back and boarding last may have their bag checked free.
http://bit.ly/cODG2p

DEPARTURE FEES
Several countries, such as New Zealand, charge a fee when you leave the country. In some countries, such as Canada, the fee only applies if your departure is from that airport; if you are connecting from a domestic flight, there is no fee. The charge may equal $10 to $20 USD. Make sure you have enough local currency to pay the departure tax.

SOME AIR TAXES COST MORE THAN THEY COLLECT
Several countries have tested Air Passenger Duty. In 2009, the Netherlands followed Belgium in abandoning its APD because although it raised $420m USD (£266m) in one year, the Dutch reckoned the loss to the wider economy as a result of the tax was over $1.5bn (£950m).

Same in the UK. If a family of four from Australia visited Britain or vice versa they would pay out around $537 (£340) in APD before they have even boarded the plane.

"The airports didn't like it, the airlines didn't like it, and tourists didn't like it. Dutch travelers were very quick to go over to Belgium or Germany and jump on a budget airline for half the price on their holiday. So abolishing the tax was a win-win for everyone," explained Robin Pascoe, editor of Dutchnews.nl.
http://bbc.in/evqv6z

CANADIAN AIRPORTS LOWER OR FREEZE FEES TO BE COMPETITIVE

The tax for a single international flight originating from Canada was $17 last year. It's now $25.91. The domestic flight fee has risen from $4.90 to $7.48.

By contrast, American air travelers are required to pay just $2.50 USD per boarding, up to a maximum of two boardings per trip. Hence Vancouver's difficulties in competing with Seattle.

http://bit.ly/bjIck9, http://bit.ly/93ambf

E. Tipping

EUROPEAN RESTAURANT AND TAXI TIPPING GUIDE
See http://bit.ly/967tIq

GREENBERG ON TIPPING
When and where.

Peter Greenberg gives advice on the popular travel topic of tipping. Different countries have different customs for gratuities. Read to ensure you don't offend anyone.
http://www.youtube.com/watch?v=tuJFYjaePl4

F. Airline Frequent Flyer & Hotel Stay Programs

TOO MANY FREQUENT-FLYER POINTS?
Are you accumulating points faster than you can spend them? Some airlines let you trade points for

merchandise: jewelry, travel items, kitchen utensils, tools, and more. For example, see http://bit.ly/b8Es20

Click on Redeem Miles for Mileage Plus Merchandise. See your airline website.

FREQUENT FLYER PROGRAMS RAISE COST OF FARES
Frequent flyer programs have driven up the cost of a ticket by about five per cent for Coach and nine per cent for Business Class. http://bit.ly/d14vhY

YOUR AIRLINE COULD SELL-OFF ITS FREQUENT-FLYER PROGRAM
How will that affect your bank of points? See http://bit.ly/cvWDHk

ANOTHER WAY TO REDEEM LUFTHANSA *MILES & MORE* AWARD POINTS
Passengers may pay their airport taxes and charges, plus the fuel surcharge, and for their flight awards by redeeming award miles. This applies for flight awards issued for Lufthansa, Austrian Airlines and selected Miles & More airline partners within Europe. Award Miles can be used online or by calling the carrier.

YOU CAN'T ALWAYS GET WHAT YOU WANT
Redeeming airline rewards can be a challenge if you're looking for first- or business-class seats. Patience and timing are essential
http://bit.ly/9nUesl

KEEPING TRACK OF YOUR AIR MILES
MileTracker keeps you current with all the details of your frequent flyer and loyalty programs. Real-time updates ensure that your data stays fresh and accurate. http://bit.ly/az0Qpt

G. Airfares

GOOGLE AIR?
Google revealed that it intends to buy ITA Software for $700 million USD.

The Cambridge, Mass., company--founded in 1996 by Massachusetts Institute of Technology computer scientists--provides airline flight information software.

Its data is used on a host of websites like Kayak, Orbitz, Expedia.com, TripAdvisor and Microsoft's (MSFT, Fortune 500) Bing, as well as a number of airlines' websites. Nearly half of airline tickets are now bought online, according to Google.
Google intends to use ITA's software and engineering expertise to make it easier to find flight information online, including pricing and ticket availability.
http://bit.ly/dpPGDD

CAUTION ON BOOKING TICKETS AND FLIGHTS ONLINE
--Michael A. Podolinsky, Singapore.

My bride and I traveled from Singapore to Brisbane last December for a 9-day holiday, sourcing the best deals online using Singapore travel sites (all in Singapore dollars). A click or two later, I was on Travelocity and they were $5 each way cheaper than the previous site on air tickets so I thought I was saving another $20. They had a link to book packages that included a good deal on an oceanfront suite and another for a rental car which were slightly better than the other sites. When we returned from the trip and got the card statement, we were SHOCKED to find out charges were in U.S. dollars, not Singapore dollars.

Travelocity never said which currency (not even in confirmation documentation) and as the prices were almost identical to the others quoting in SGD, I mistakenly thought it was SGD.

It took 3 months to clear up before they refunded the difference on the airline and hotel. The Australian rental car turned out to be AUD and they would not refund the difference.

MORAL 1: When booking online, be absolutely sure which currency you are quoted.

MORAL 2: Consider going to (for example) zuji.com.sg or zuji.com.au or whatever country you are going to and find out if it's cheaper on their site because it's in local currency. e.g.: Book a return ticket between KL, Malaysia and Singapore in KL, it's the SAME $ amount but in MYR VS. SGD. That is HALF PRICE.

H. Air Travel Insurance.

There are several types of insurance available to the air traveler.

You can get coverage for lost or delayed baggage, trip cancellation, medical evacuations, waivers on pre-existing conditions, medical and dental expenses, accidental death and dismemberment, and everything in between.

First, check the coverage provided by your various credit cards.

AIR TRAVEL ACCIDENT INSURANCE
If a plane crash happens and you are injured or killed in it, your family will be compensated. Usually, the coverage is about $100,000.

The air travel insurance policy is terminated once you get off the plane. Remember that the insurance policy can be used only in commercial flights and not for private air travel. The policy must be purchased before you board the plane. The cheapest policy can be bought for about $12 USD for each individual but there are also family rates available.
http://bit.ly/bf0kdK

TRIP INTERUPTION INSURANCE
Trip Interruption insurance will protect you against flight delays, which could end up costing you extra money on hotel rooms, food, flight cancellations, and other things that are out of your control.
http://www.top10travelinsurance.com/

MEDICAL EVACUATION INSURANCE

Medical emergency? Domestic air medical evacuation averages $10,000 to $20,000, and internationally, it can exceed $75,000. But not with the medical evacuation service from MedjetAssist. As a member, if you are hospitalized 150 miles or more away from home, MedjetAssist will arrange for medical transfer to the hospital of your choice--at no additional charge. No transportation cost limitations. No pre-existing condition exclusions. Just peace of mind each and every time you travel.

MedjetAssist lets you decide which hospital will be your final destination. Plus, there's no medical-necessity clause. If you are hospitalized, they will be there for you—regardless of the nature of your illness or injury. Annual membership is $250. http://bit.ly/fFZj4i

Also see http://www.travelguard.com/

☺ **Humor**

YOU KNOW IT'S A "NO FRILLS" AIRLINE WHEN...

They don't sell tickets, they sell chances.

All the insurance machines in the terminal are sold out.
Before the flight, the passengers get together and elect a pilot.

You cannot board the plane unless you have the exact change.

Before you took off, the flight attendant tells you to fasten your Velcro.

The Captain asks all the passengers to chip in a little for fuel.

When they pull the steps away, the plane starts rocking.

The Captain yells at the ground crew to get the cows off the runway.

You ask the Captain how often their planes crash and he says,
"Just once."

No movie. Don't need one. Your life keeps flashing before your eyes.

You see a man with a gun, but he's demanding to be let off the plane.

All the planes have both a bathroom and a chapel.

SOUTHWEST AIRLINES FEES COMMERCIAL
"Fees don't fly with us."
http://www.youtube.com/watch?v=hjUlrirW480

FEES
With all the discounted fares, the airlines are coming up with new ways to make money. For example, it now costs $3.50 for your kid to ride the baggage conveyor.

Chapter Thirteen
Communication in the Air & on the Road
Electrical, Telephone, etc.

A. Electrical
B. Telephone
C. WiFi
D. Email

A. Electrical

ADAPTERS vs CONVERTERS
Adapters change the plug.
Converters change the voltage.

Most appliances today are dual voltage. This short informative video shows you which adaptors and converters you will need.
http://bit.ly/g3O6XW

ELECTRICAL ADAPTERS—WORLDWIDE
Power adapters are even more important to the traveling professional speaker. In addition to appliances such as shavers and hairdryers, we need to run our computers and projectors. See the adapter illustrations at
http://bit.ly/gnnEch

There are individual adapter plugs and multiple all-in-one adapters. The all-in-one adapters do not always work everywhere. A wide range of adapters can be found in most airport shops.

Always carry a three-way plug from home. That way you will be able to plug into the individual-country adapter and power more than one of your appliances the same time. Remember, a computer and a projector each require a power source.

WORLDWIDE ELECTRICAL AND TELEPHONE INFORMATION
Steve Kropla's *Help For Worldwide Travelers*, has a comprehensive listing of worldwide electrical and phone info. You can search for information such as: International City Codes, Electric Plug Types, Television Standards, Mobile Phone Guides and more.
http://www.kropla.com/

B. Telephone

FACTOID
Today 30% of all mobile devices are Smartphones (iPhone, Blackberry, Android, Palm) and by the end of 2011 this percentage will double.

COUNTRY-TELEPHONE CODE LOOKUP
It will also list the time at the place you are calling. See
http://www.countrycallingcodes.com/

DOES YOUR TELEPHONE LISTING MAKE YOU APPEAR INTERNATIONAL?
--Dan Poynter, USA.

Each country or area has a unique "country code" for dialing. The UK is 44, Australia is 65 and 1 covers the U.S., Canada and some Caribbean islands.

Most people know to list a full ten-digit number for North American numbers. You will appear to be worldlier if you list 11 numbers. For example: +1-805-968-7277.

The + is for the dial-out-of-this-country signal. In North America, it is 011, in some other countries it is 0 or 01; confusing. Most mobile phones will prefix the dial-out number if you hold down the 0 for about 3 seconds. Hence adding + to your number. You do not have to look up the country code.

List the +, etc. on all your contact areas: Website, business card, brochures, etc. Appear international.

FREE TELEPHONE CALLS.
--Frank Furness, UK.

Introduction to Skype.
http://bit.ly/be371y

SKYPE
While few North American travelers know about Skype, most international travelers rely on it. With Skype, you can make VOIP (Internet) calls to other Skype subscribers free. Calls to landline phones cost

about two-cents/minute USD. All you need is a headset plugged into your desktop or notebook computer using high-speed Internet access. Subscribing is very easy. See http://www.skype.com/download/

SKYPE UPDATES. Significant changes have been made to your favorite free telephone system. Get the new features by updating the program now.
See http://www.Skype.com
Skype>Help>Check for Updates
Do it now.

PHONE: INFORMATION AND DIALER
Put this number into your mobile-phone favorites and you won't have to dial numbers in North America. 1-800-GOOG411. Speed-dial Google Info to get the number and then the system will dial the number for you. No charge and very handy when driving.

MOBILE PHONE COVERAGE IN THE US
Going to a remote area? Wondering if your cell phone and computer data card will work there?

Go to http://bit.ly/9UQHqO
And type in the ZIP Code. The site will tell you the number of towers and rate the coverage for AT&T, Verizon, Sprint, T-Mobile and Nextel. Then see the coverage maps for each carrier.

MOBILE PHONE JAMMING DEVICES
The buyers include owners of cafes and hair salons, hoteliers, professional speakers, theater operators,

bus drivers and, increasingly, commuters on public transportation. See
http://nyti.ms/bTaWQr

One supplier is
http://phonejammer.com/
Make an online search for more suppliers.

GETTING THROUGH TO CUSTOMER SERVICE ON THE PHONE
Are you tired of wading through "push 1 for this and press 2 for that?"

For a cheat sheet for many companies in the US, Canada, and the UK, with numbers to push to get to a human representative, see
http://www.gethuman.com/world.html

THERE ARE TWO KINDS OF FREQUENT FLYERS
Those with an iPhone and
those with a few months left on their contract. (:

IN-FLIGHT VOICE-CALL STATS REVEALED
AeroMobile, whose mobile connectivity solution is in place on 60% of Emirates' in-service fleet, says that more than 11,000 voice calls were made/received to equipped Emirates aircraft in February 2010 alone.

The longest call made from an aircraft was 65min on a Dubai-Accra flight on 11 October 2009. The highest number of calls made from an aircraft was 82 on a Bombay-Dubai flight on 20 September 2009.
http://bit.ly/a3Tq1G

MOBILE PHONES BEING USED ON PLANES
--Carnegie Mellon University

Even though cell phone use during flight is banned, on average 1 to 4 cell phone calls are made from every commercial flight in the Northeast U.S.
http://bit.ly/a4ikjC

MOBILE PHONE USE ON PLANES IS COVERED BY THE FCC NOT THE FAA
Federal Communications Commission (FCC) rules prohibit the use of cellular phones using the 800 MHz frequency and other wireless devices on airborne aircraft. This ban was put into place to prevent cell phone towers from being overwhelmed by thousands of phones moving at 500 miles per hour searching for signals.
http://bit.ly/f1XBl9, http://bit.ly/dXpi8R

THE iPHONE MUTE BUTTON
When placing an important call on your iPhone, press for another screen page. When calling, the Mute button is shown; your cheek can easily touch it and shut off your mic.

The problem is that you will not know you are not transmitting until you are told. This can be especially embarrassing on a radio interview. You could be talking for minutes, not realizing that you are "cut off."

MOBILE PHONE RANGE

Cell phone operating distances depend on many things such as distance, operating system, terrain and other interference, power of the phone, etc.

Distance from the cell-tower is the most critical. It is rare that a cell phone will find a signal when the plane is below 10,000 feet. That is why you hear phones go off on final approach (landing at airports.) They just picked up a signal from a tower.

C. WiFi

WiFi HOTSPOTS

Get on line. Find hotspots when you travel; pay and free. See

WiFi Zone Finder: http://wi-fi.jiwire.com/
WiFi Free Spot: http://www.wififreespot.com/
WiFi 411: http://www.wifi411.com/
Use Google Maps to find free hotspots:
http://www.gwifi.net/

FREE WiFi IN AIRPORTS.

Many Airport authorities are adding Free Wi-Fi high-speed Internet access as an amenity for travelers. Some offer access in the entire airport while others may limit access to specified terminals or waiting areas. In addition, many airline club lounges may have their own free access available. See
http://wififreespot.com/airport.html

FIND ELECTRICAL POWER AND Wi-Fi IN AIRPORTS WORLDWIDE

From Addis Ababa, Ethiopia (ADD) to Zurich, Switzerland (ZRH). http://bit.ly/bh9q6M

THE MOST AND LEAST WIRED AIRLINES AND AIRPORTS

Air travelers are fed up with being disconnected for hours. Some airlines and airports are responding, offering email connections, IM, and live TV. But others are woefully behind. See http://bit.ly/aq9ETY

BEWARE OF FREE WiFi IN PUBLIC PLACES
--Peter Shankman, USA.

A program titled *FireSheep*, a *Firefox* extension, allows people to see who's connecting to various sites that don't encrypt their http login cookies, like Facebook, Evernote, Yahoo, Amazon, Dropbox, Gowalla, Twitter, WordPress, and others, to name a very limited few.

Once people see who's connected, it's a simple matter of double clicking on your name, and they are logged into your account, as you. People can get access to your accounts and even delete them.

Avoid open Wi-Fi networks where it's possible for others on the network to sniff the traffic your computer's sending and receiving to various sites. If you must use open Wi-Fi, try to use an https connection. http://bit.ly/cHSrpH, http://bit.ly/9sz9Z1

Wi-Fi BY THE HOUR

Need temporary airport WiFi access but don't want to pay for an entire month of access? Boingo Wireless, operator of 125,000-plus global hotspots in airports, hotels, cafes, and coffee shops, has one alternative for iPhone, iPad, and iPod touch owners.

Buy one-hour credits for $1.99 USD at the iTunes Store.

Boingo's standard offering is $7.95 for a month of coverage.

You'll need to download a free Boingo WiFi-Credits app from iTunes, which comes with a $1.99 credit. A 10-credit package is $19.99 and includes an 11th credit free. http://bit.ly/akImGk

HOTSPOT SPEEDS FOR EMAIL, WEB SURFING AND SKYPE

As you travel, check the Internet connection speed; not all Internet hotspots are fast enough. By measuring the download and upload rate you are able to accurately judge your current line throughput or internet connection speed.

Speed testing. Look for a download speed of at least 1 Mbps and an upload speed of at least 400 Kbps. If the hotspot is not too busy, you should get reasonable connection. See
http://www.speakeasy.net/speedtest/

Another test site:
http://www.pcpitstop.com/internet/default.asp

FRUSTRATED BY LOSING HOTEL WiFi CONNECTIONS?

Most of the time, wireless connections are stable enough, but every once in a while, you may get a bad connection that keeps dropping out on you. In this case, there are a few steps you can take to ensure a more solid connection. See http://bit.ly/b6NaBy

WiFi ON PLANES

Look for signs in the planes and for notices in the seat-back pockets. Charges may vary with the length of the flight and type of device you are using. Smart phones and PDAs may cost less than computer use.

Once you register with the provider, signing on in the future wil be faster.

Check your flight for WiFi availability.
http://haswifi.com/

WIFI ON PLANES:

A satellite-based system allows global (over ocean) coverage.

A tower system only works over land such as the US or Europe.

WiFi FINDER APP FOR THE iPHONE

http://www.jiwire.com/iphone
And see the App Store.

INCREASING YOUR WiFi SIGNAL

Do you need a stronger wireless signal or greater network access? Here is a simple hack to extend the range of your wireless card.

Video with Mark Erickson.
http://bit.ly/gvis1f

D. Email

SIGNATURES ON EMAILS

If you have a business card, your email messages need a signature.
You want people to know who you are, what you do, and how to find you.

The signature is a block of information people add to the end of their messages. It is simple to set up and it's free. Whatever email program you are using, click on HELP and type in signature. The instructions will pop up. The first time might take you 15 minutes. Changes will take far less.

Many businesspeople know about signatures but some still do not.

If you want to add a photo to your signature--of yourself, company logo, and/or your book cover, open Outlook and go to
Tools\Options\Mail format\Signatures\New\type in "signature."
Then add your contact info.
Next, Right click\Insert\Image.

And select a photo from the directory on you hard drive to insert.

vMAIL/VIDEO eMAIL.
--Terry Brock, USA.

Why type when you can email a recorded message?

Get the Logitech QuickCam® for Notebooks Deluxe or Quick Cam Fusion camera. Load the Logitech software. Record your video message and attach it to your email. No headset required; the microphone is built-in to the camera. See http://bit.ly/9Qe4wF

Chapter Fourteen
Equipment & Technology

A. Computers
B. PowerPoint
C. Batteries
D. Public-Address Systems
E. PDAs
F. Programs & Apps
G. Video

TRAVEL GADGETS
A Peter Greenberg video on things you can carry to make the trip easier and more fun.
http://www.youtube.com/watch?v=2jqQKlHvfJ0
http://bit.ly/eMqvDa,
http://bit.ly/fs6foJ

TEN USEFUL GADGETS FOR MOBILE COMPUTING
http://bit.ly/9f5Oh8

A. Computers

SMALLER COMPUTERS FOR TRAVEL
People who travel regularly need lighter-weight, lower-volume, travel items. One place to save space and weight is your computer.

Smaller computers take up less space on airplane seat tables and will fit into the smaller hotel-room safes.

CONSIDERING A NETBOOK?

These small, inexpensive PCs are nice for the air traveler but be aware that many do not have the power to properly run *PowerPoint*. Test before you buy.

KEYBOARD SHORTCUTS FOR MS-*WORD*

See
http://bit.ly/d8TC5B

FASCINATING COMPUTER SHORTCUTS MOST PEOPLE DON'T KNOW.

http://nyti.ms/aEIjHy

HELP! I'VE SPILLED COFFEE ON MY LAPTOP

You can save the computer if you act quickly. Solutions depend on whether you are on battery or AC power. See
http://bit.ly/cRdJlP

SOME MICE PROHIBITED ON COMMERCIAL AIRLINERS

Electronic devices capable of transmitting an electrical signal may not be used on airliners over most countries.

Cordless mice transmit with Bluetooth technology to enable the mouse to communicate with the computer. Therefore the use of cordless mice is not permitted.
The prohibition applies to all Bluetooth devices, including headphones.

B. PowerPoint

NOTEBOOK-PROJECTOR SETUP PROBLEMS

You are dressed, rehearsed, ready-to-go and the projector fails. Your speech begins in six minutes. What to do. Breathe.

Some things to try when PowerPoint is not projecting.
http://bit.ly/corKjN
http://bit.ly/96gx80

HOW TO REALLY USE POWERPOINT
--Roger Harrop, UK.

It is a tool for *supplementing* your speech.
http://bit.ly/ceIlcX

USING YOUR iPHONE TO CONTROL PROJECTED KEYNOTE PRESENTATIONS

Amazing the control you can have over your Mac. See
http://bit.ly/fJPElO
Scroll down to Control Keynote Remotely to see the video.

POWERPOINT TIP
--Steve Hughes, USA.

When in Slide-Show mode, press F1 for a list of keystroke shortcuts.

MULTIMEDIA TIP
Automating slides for keynotes
--Adele Landauer, Germany.

When you're presenting a keynote and want your slides on the screen for just a few seconds each, you have a choice. The remote you are using may have a button for "black" or you could go over to the computer keyboard and press the B key. Either one requires extra steps and takes your mind off of your verbal delivery.

An automated alternative is to set up the show so that when you click on a slide it comes up for a predetermined time, such as 5 seconds, and then the screen goes black. This way, you only click once, the slide appears, and you can continue your delivery, knowing that after a few seconds the next picture will disappear.

Naturally, this is rarely a good system for content-filled breakout presentations.

In training programs, the audience often concentrates on the slides. For keynote speeches we want them to concentrate on the speaker.

POWERPOINT TYPE SIZING CHART
--Dave Paradi, Canada.
http://bit.ly/gqV4lN

POWERPOINT COLOR CONTRAST CALCULATOR
http://bit.ly/eVp1eq

COUNTDOWN CLOCKS
Alert your audience to how much time is left before the program begins and when they are expected back from the break.
Import a countdown clock into your PowerPoint show.
http://www.HahnTech.com
http://www.trialtheater.com/countdown/

POWERPOINT TIP
--Carlton C. Casler, *Presentation Excellence*, USA.

Put a "break" slide in the number one position.

Then, if your slideshow is running slower than you anticipated and your audience needs a break, all you have to do is press the number 1 on your computer keyboard.

ILLUSTRATIONS FOR YOUR POWERPOINT PRESENTATIONS
Clip art, photos, line drawings, icons, sounds and more.
http://www.ClipArt.com

PHOTO SOURCES FOR YOUR POWERPOINT
--Beverly Babb, CAE, Beverly@nsaspeaker.org, USA.

When creating PPT slides for international presentations, you may be looking for photos of local places and local faces. These sites allow presenters to inexpensively customize their slides visually to complement their customized text. Terms of use vary and are posted on each site.

www.flickr.com
www.fotolia.com
www.imageafter.com
www.inmagine.com
www.istockphoto.com/
www.morguephotos.com/
www.photos.com
www.photospin.com
www.shutterstock.com

C. Batteries

DEAD BATTERIES

As mobile electronics become more powerful and multifunctional, the battery life of portable devices becomes shorter and shorter.

Unfortunately, business travelers can't guarantee an AC outlet will always be available to recharge their laptops, mobile phones, or PDAs. The difference between whether or not you receive an important call or email may rely on your carrying a secondary source of power. If you travel with only one portable device, a second battery is a viable solution, but at $25 to $200 apiece, purchasing numerous backup batteries may not be cost-effective. For alternatives, see http://bit.ly/94ktkB

UNIVERSAL PHONE CHARGERS COMING

A consortium of 17 mobile phone manufacturers and cellular phone companies say they have agreed on a standard for a universal charger for mobile devices. A one-size-fits-all charger may be ready by 2012. But neither Apple (iPhone, iPad) nor Research in Motion (Blackberry) have signed on.

REDUCE POWER CORD CLUTTER BY CHARGING YOUR GADGETS VIA USB
If you're running out of power outlets for plugging in all those chargers for your MP3 players, phones, and other portable gadgets, a solution may be to charge multiple devices through a powered USB hub instead. This doesn't work with every device (check the manual) but many devices will charge this way—even when the computer is dark (on standby). Here's a video about it on CNET:
http://bit.ly/g6Yhbh

D. Public Address Systems

COULD THAT AUDIO BUZZ IN THE PA SYSTEM BE COMING FROM THE BLACKBERRY IN YOUR POCKET?
Is there a hum every few minutes? Your mobile phone could be too close to your mic.

GSM Phones are reportedly guiltier than CDMA devices. See http://bit.ly/9MXmpu

E. PDAs

PDAs ARE PERFECT FOR AIR TRAVEL
Multifunction devices eliminate carrying several electronic toys. With them you can send/receive email and text messages, take photos, make Web

searches, keep your address book, maintain your calendar, read eBooks, listen to audio, make Skype calls, and much more.

The iPhone has more than 250,000 apps available. Many good PDAs make travel easier and more fun. Some are currency converters, ATM/cash machine locators, taxi finders, airline seat maps, airport gate maps, etc. See the Apple App Store.

eBOOKS AND OTHER ELECTRONIC DEVICES NOT PERMITTED ON SOUTH AFRICAN AIRWAYS
--Dan Poynter, USA.

The Civil Aviation Authority in South Africa prohibits the use in flight of any device capable of transmitting a signal, even when switched to "flight mode."

The rule reads as follows: "The use of any cellular telephone functions including 'Blackberry' and 'flight mode' is strictly prohibited."

Besides being grammatically confusing, the rule has been misinterpreted by flight crews. On a flight from Johannesburg to Washington, the announced safety instructions included the following: "Flight Mode is not to be activated at any time."

Whoever drafted this airline instruction does not understand what flight mode is.

And, reading eBooks and listening to music are not "cellular-telephone functions."

While the airline refers inquiries to the Civil Aviation Authority, the CAA does not reply to requests for clarification.
See http://bit.ly/hlS5hj

DEALING WITH A CRASHED PDA
PDAs and Smartphones aren't exempt from the freezes and glitches that plague notebooks. A bad software installation can trip up your device, and operating system quirks can wreak havoc at inopportune times.

Unlike notebooks, your handheld has very few removable parts, which means you can't solve problems by swapping out defective hardware with a new component.
http://bit.ly/9QNRhR

F. Programs & Apps

FACTOID
The mobile App economy will total $17.5 billion USD by 2012 and downloads across all handsets will soar from 7 billion in 2009 to 50 billion in 2012.

WHAT APP BRINGS THE SECURITY?
Plenty of Web sites offer mobile app reviews, but WhatApp? (www.whatapp.org), from Stanford University, tells you how private, open, and secure apps are in Web, Web Browsers, Mobile Platforms, and Social Networks categories.

Ratings involve combining "traditional consumer reporting and review tools with wikis and news feeds."
https://whatapp.org/

GOOGLE FEATURES FOR TRAVELERS
Google has some handy algorithms in their service, which allow travelers to quickly locate particular and specific types of information.

a. Movies
In order to locate reviews and show times for films playing near you, type "movies" or the name of a current film into the Google search box. If you have already saved your location on a previous search, or if you are logged into a Google account, the top search result will display show times for nearby theaters for the movie you entered.

b. Flight Status
To view the flight status for arriving and departing US airline flights, enter the name of the airline and the flight number into the Google search box. Airport delays and details can be found by typing in the name of the city or three-letter airport code, followed by the word "airport."

c. Definitions
In order to quickly find the definition of a word, simply type
"define: word" in the search box. Google will then provide the definition of the word.

d. Weather

To see the weather for many U.S. and worldwide cities, type, "weather" followed by the city and state, U.S. Zip Code, or city and country.
Google will provide a current weather forecast.

e. Measurement Conversion Calculator
Convert height, weight, and volume measurements. Just enter the desired conversion into the search box and Google will calculate the conversion.

f. Patent Search
Enter the word "patent" followed by the U.S. patent number into the Google search box; Google will display the details of that particular patent.

g. Related Websites
Google will display web pages that contain similar content.
Include "related:" followed by a website address in the Google search box for a listing of similar websites.

h. Population & Unemployment Rates
For population and unemployment numbers of U.S. states and counties, type "population" or "unemployment rate" followed by a state or county. Then click through to a page that lets you compare different locations.

i. Indexed Pages
When "site:" is entered in the Google search box, followed by a domain name, the search engine locates all documents within a specific domain, including all of its sub-domains. This is an easy way

to get a rough idea of the number of pages indexed for a given domain.

j. Calculator
Type a math problem into the Google search box, and Google will calculate the answer. Google acts as a calculator when mathematical calculation is presented. Google recognizes the following mathematical symbols: addition (+), subtraction (-), multiplication (*), division (/), to the power of (^), and square root of a number (sort)

k. Measurement Conversion Calculator
Convert height, weight, and volume measurements. Just enter the desired conversion into the search box and Google will calculate the conversion.

l. Spell Check
Google automatically checks whether your query uses the most common spelling of a given word. If Google thinks there may be an alternate or better spelling, it will be listed as: "Did you mean: (alternate spelling)?

m. Current Time Worldwide
To see the current time in any city around the world, type "time" and the name of the city. Google will display the current time for that city.
e.g.: time Santa Barbara

n. Convert Currency
Enter the conversion you would like to see performed in the Google search box, and Google will provide the

current rate, e.g.: convert 94 Singapore Dollars to US Dollars

o. Track Shipments
Shipments can easily be tracked using Google simply by entering the tracking number for your UPS, FedEx, or USPS package directly into the Google search box. Google will return the tracking results and status of the shipment.

p. Earthquake Activity
Google even tracks earthquake activity. Enter "earthquake" followed by the city and state or U.S. Zip Code into the Google search box to see the seismic activity in a specific region.

q. Linked Websites
Which sites are linked to your site? Put "link:" followed by a URL in the Google search box. The search results will include a listing of web pages that contain links to the specified URL.

r. Population
To see population trends and unemployment rates of U.S. states and counties, type "population" or "unemployment rate" followed by a state or country. Click through to a page to compare different locations.

s. Stock Quotes
Keep an eye on the changing stock market. To see current market data for a given company or fund, simply type the ticker symbol into the Google search

box. The resulting webpage displays financial data from the Google Finance service.

Google Mobile App has a voice search feature. Press the microphone icon and ask for what you want. For example, say "Mexican restaurants in Singapore" and up pops a list. Press on a listing and you will get the complete address, restaurant reviews, and a map.

Say "Taxis in Brisbane, Australia" and get a list with contact information.

Of course, you may type in your request but the voice search is fast and easy. There is no need to train the PDA to your voice.
No charge for the App.

iPHONE APPS FOR TRAVEL AND MEETINGS
One of the major benefits of the iPhone is the availability of more than 250,000 applications from the App store. Frequent flyers may customize their multifunction PDA for travel and meetings. Here are some Apps our colleagues have found useful. See http://bit.ly/aE0Q4O

Travel Kit
Several functions: world clock, currency exchange, destination fact book, unit converter, flight mate, tip calculator, flashlight (torch), post card maker, and translator. This multifunction app enables you to eliminate some individual-function apps.

Air Mile Calculator
Enter the cities in your itinerary and the app will total the air miles.

Google (Voice Activated)
The Google search engine you love now has Voice Search. E.g., say the name of a hotel and up will pop a map and full contact information. Free.

Kindle for iPhone
All of Amazon's Kindle eBooks may be read on the iPhone and iPod touch. This free application gives you access to the Amazon store where you can search for Kindle books.

You may read the first 20% of any book at no charge. Then, if you like the book, click "Buy." Your account will be debited and the rest of the book will download in less than 20 seconds.

You can carry thousands of books on your iPhone. Turn airport waits, flight delays, and queues into a benefit. Pick up your iPhone and continue reading.

ATM/Cash Machine Hunter
Most travelers find the best exchange rates to be from ATMs. This App finds your location via GPS and lists the nearest ATMs with addresses and distance.

iHandy Carpenter. Five professional tools in one App. Surface level, plumb bob, bubble level bar, steel protractor, steel ruler, and inclinometer. Free.

IHUD. Airplane Heads-Up Display. Uses the 3Gs GPS and accelerometer data to display heading, speed, altitude, vertical speed, slip/skid, etc. $5.99

G-Park. Find where you parked your car. G-Park uses GPS for location. $.99
1. Park your car and touch the Park Me button.
2. Get lost.
3. Hit the Where Did I Park button.

GPS Thermometer provides local temperature in Celsius and Fahrenheit. Using the GPS feature, it finds your location and reports the temperature. It also provides a map to show where the temperature is reported. 99 cents USD. Other thermometers are also available from the App store.

Another way to find the local temperature is to use the Google mobile app, described above. For example, say "weather in Cape Town, South Africa." and all the details will appear.

Bump
--Craig Rispin, Australia.
Now you can exchange business cards by holding your iPhone in your hand and bumping knuckles with another person.

Bump makes swapping contact information and photos as simple as bumping two iPhones together. No typing in or searching the list for the right person, no mistakes.

Contact information is saved directly into your address book, and photos are saved directly into your Camera Roll. Perfect for exchanging virtual business cards or just exchanging information with colleagues. See Bump in the iTunes store.

Tips & Tricks
Bite-size tips for busy people: learn hidden shortcuts, how to fix your problem and maximize your battery life. Learn tips and tricks to increase your typing speed and a heap of secret features to wow other iPhone and iPod touch owners. Not a manual; just screen after screen of helpful tips. See *Tips & Tricks* at the iTunes store.

Air Canada
Air Canada is the first North American airline to release an Apple(R) iPhone(TM)/iPod touch(R) application. The free App makes it convenient for travelers with Apple devices to retrieve electronic boarding passes, track flight information in real-time, receive notification of itinerary changes and obtain other details about Air Canada flights.

Airline Seat Guide
Look up the seating charts for airliners worldwide. Categorized by carrier. Especially useful when changing itineraries at an airport. Similar to *Seat Guru*.
$1.99 USD.

Quotationary is a dictionary of quotations that contains more than 32,000 famous and inspirational sayings from thousands of different authors. It is a great reference for any professional speaker.

Quotations are stored on the device so Internet access is not required. $3.99 USD.

GPS navigation with voice

Both AT&T and Tom Tom offer Apps for GPS navigation with turn-by-turn voice institutions. Now, when your taxi driver does not know the area, you can turn on your iPhone and get the same type of driving directions you get in your own car. See the App Store. The offers differ so check them both.

Rocket Taxi

This App checks your location with GPS and lists nearby taxi companies with distances. Just select one, press on it and a call will be initiated to the cab company.

Shazam

Identify music anywhere: from the radio, TV, film, or in a store by simply holding your iPhone toward the music and tapping "tag."

In the tag results you will view the lyrics, read track and album reviews and artist biographies, and lists of other music from the artists.

Trailguru

Capture your next walk, run, ride, hike, biking trip, or any outdoor activity. This is a pedometer using your iPhone's integrated GPS.

In the midst of your activity, Trailguru displays the vital statistics of the distance traveled, duration, pace/speed, elevation, and latitude and longitude. You are also able to visualize the activity on an integrated map and easily take geo-tagged photos for automatic upload. Once you upload the activity to the Trailguru website, you'll be able to visualize your outing on Google Earth and Google Maps, keep track of how much you've done over time with web-based reporting and learn about other places you can explore.

Decibel Meter
How much noise is there in that auditorium, sleeping room or airplane? Now you can measure the decibel sound pressure level using the built-in mic in your iPhone. It will show you the average decibel reading as well as the peak decibel reading. Then it interprets the level of the sound. Choose between level meter and graph view. $1.99.

Skype
Most international professional travelers are already using Skype, especially for international calls. Calls to other Skype users are free, Skype calls to land lines are less than two-euro cents per minute, and Skype can include video. The best part is you can use Skype from your handheld PDA; you are not tethered to a wall.

Many international hotels offer free WiFi and many more offer free WiFi in the lobby area.

If you already have a Skype account, you may log on using your iPhone. If you don't already have a Skype account, sign up and put in a small deposit; pay in advance for your calls.

Load the App into your computer and iPhone. Use your computer to sign up for Skype. Now, you're ready to make calls.

IPHONE APPS FOR AIR TRAVELERS
Without ever leaving your iPhone, you can check for delays, find the best seat on your flight, learn facts about your aircraft, and find your departure gate at the airport. http://bit.ly/ia4NCp

TRAVEL APPS FOR THE iPHONE
--Erwin van Lun, The Netherlands.

See the descriptions on YouTube.
http://www.youtube.com/watch?v=afiLiI-7mr8

EIGHT iPHONE APPS FOR ROAD WARRIORS
Now that Smartphones have become virtual pocket-sized notebooks, business travelers have more reasons than ever to carry around a Smartphone featuring great applications, such as the iPhone.
http://bit.ly/cAvzsU

CALENDAR GRID PDFs FOR 2010
Print out your own calendar. Seven formats to choose from. http://bit.ly/ccBPuW

G. Video

DEMO/PROMO VIDEOS WITH GREEN SCREEN

Making a video and need some exotic backdrops? It can be done with green screen technology—without leaving town. See http://bit.ly/iaJzRH

BTW, in some parts of the world, such as Singapore, a blue screen is used.

Chapter Fifteen
Maps, Distance Calculators, & News

WORLD MAPPER
Maps of the world redrawn according to specific activities. Fascinating statistics explained and displayed in a new way. See
http://www.worldmapper.org/
http://www.worldmapper.org/atozindex.html

CIA MAPS & PUBLICATIONS
The Central Intelligence Agency's Maps and Publications section is a listing of all unclassified maps and publications available to the public for purchase from GPO and/or NTIS.

CITY DISTANCE CALCULATOR. Find the distance between any two cities. See
http://www.geobytes.com/CityDistanceTool.htm

AIRLINE MILE CALCULATOR
How many miles will you get between any two cities? See
http://www.usatoday.com/travel/flights/miles/calculator.htm

EUROPEAN GEOGRAPHY QUIZ ONLINE.
http://bit.ly/cRfkSu

READ THE FRONT PAGE OF YOUR HOME NEWSPAPER WHILE TRAVELING.
Get instant access to 450 newspapers from 70 countries in 37 languages. The front page is free; if you want the entire paper, there is a subscription fee. See
http://bit.ly/gFpv9c

NEWSPAPER FRONT PAGES--WORLDWIDE
--Joe Sherren, Canada.

The Newseum displays daily newspaper front pages in their original, unedited form. Check the site before your next trip. See the major news items. Just put your mouse on a city anywhere in the world and the newspaper headlines pop up. Double click and the page gets larger....
http://bit.ly/gVFuiJ

USA TODAY SITE DEVOTED TO TRAVEL
Flight tracker, airport guides, weather, and more.
http://usat.ly/hzgKh7

Chapter Sixteen
Time & Time Zones

VIDEO EXPLANATION OF TIME ZONES
A skillful combination of animation, live photography and representational models of the Earth clearly illustrate latitude and longitude, the prime meridian and time zones.
http://bit.ly/f4ZEVm

ALL ABOUT TIME
Time zones, time, sunrise-sunset; day-night map, distance calculator and more. See
http://www.timeanddate.com/time/

WORLD CLOCK
Locate the time in cities around the world. See and bookmark this site:
http://www.timeanddate.com/worldclock/

iPHONE CLOCK
The iPhone comes with a clock. It includes a world clock, alarm clock, stopwatch, and countdown timer. Not only can you check the time in various parts of the world, now travelers do not have to carry an alarm clock.

Chapter Seventeen
Hotels

Frequent air travelers stay away overnight so here are some hotel tips.

FACTOID
There are around 50,000 hotels and nearly 5 million guestrooms in the United States. There is no count of the total numbers worldwide.

PARENT AND AFFILIATE HOTELS
Keeping your points in a minimum of hotel (chains) will help you to climb the frequent-stay status ladder faster. Once you obtain the Gold, etc. level, you may qualify for the club-level rooms, free breakfast, clubroom access, free Internet, and other perks.

But you don't have to stay in the flagship hotels; you can accrue points with their less-expensive affiliates. Here is a list of some parent hotels and their relations:

Marriott: Fairfield Inn, Renaissance Hotels, Courtyard, Residence Inn, Springhill Suites & TownePlace Suites.
Hilton: Hampton Inn, Doubletree, Conrad Hotels, Homewood Suites & Embassy Suites.
Hyatt: (All have Hyatt in their name)
Radisson: Country Inns, Park Inn, Park Plaza & Regent Int'l Hotels.

Starwood: Westin, Sheraton, Four Points, St. Regis, Luxury Collection.
Intercontinental: Crowne Plaza, Holiday Inn, Candlewood Suites, hotel INDIGO, & Staybridge Suites.
Choice Hotels: Clarion, Comfort, Quality, Sleep Inn, MainStay Suites, EconoLodge, Rodeway Inn.
Millennium: Copthorne.
Accor: Accor/Mecure, Soffitel, Novotel, Adagio, Pullman, AllSeasons, etc.

The affiliates often have free Internet and free breakfast in addition to a fitness center, business center, etc.

The more expensive hotels can be a wise buy. Most have free Internet, Clubroom access with free breakfast, free light supper, and free drinks. Compare *total* pricing when selecting a hotel.

WHAT IS NOT IN THE HOTEL BROCHURE?
A video with inside tips with Peter Greenberg/
http://bit.ly/dUSnlQ

HOTEL TIPS
Stay near the airport terminal. Airport hotels are less expensive than downtown hotels. You can take the hotel van over for early flights, minimizing traffic & weather challenges.

Book online at hotel sites to get points, upgrades, late checkouts, etc. Many travelers find they get better treatment booking directly than through a consolidator site.

Keep records on hotel, vans, etc. Review your notes on your next visit to the area.

On checking in, tear off the room number printed on the room key jacket and put it in your wallet along with the second room key. It is often difficult to remember room numbers.

Or, get the iPhone App titled Room (free). You can store the number and hotel name there.

Take the stairs at least once so you know where they are in case of an emergency.

HOTEL CHATTER
A daily web magazine with uncensored hotel reviews from all over the world. The Good, The Bad, and The Disgusting. It covers hotel deals, reviews, tips, hotels to avoid, and great hotels to stay in.

It's updated daily. They welcome traveler input. If you have something to say about a hotel stay, have a tip on finding hotel deals, have photos of a top-notch hotel, or know the perfect place for the traveler, become a member and submit your story. Or just comment on the current published stories.
http://www.hotelchatter.com/

HOTEL MIRRORS, SHOWERS AND BEDS NOT DESIGNED FOR THE TALL TRAVELER
--Alan Stevens, UK. *The Tall Traveler.*

I reckon I could tell you the maximum height of a hotel handyman. Five foot eight. That's the only explanation I can think of for the plethora of low-hung mirrors and showerheads (we'll get to beds in a minute, if you'll bear with me). In the great majority of hotels that I've stayed in around the world, showering has been a very uncomfortable experience, owing to the fact that I've had to crouch in a very undignified manner. In many cases, I've also had to genuflect in front of the mirror in order not to have to shave from memory.

As for the beds, most of them seem to be the standard six foot three, which requires a ceremonial untucking of all the sheets every night, in order to fit (just) under the covers. Oddly enough, hotel beds seem to be getting wider, which may mean that at some point I can move the pillows to the edge and sleep at ninety degrees (if you see what I mean).

So, I say "Tall Travelers Unite!" Let's fill in all those feedback sheets in hotel bedrooms and demand higher mirrors and showers, as well as longer beds. We have nothing to lose but the pains in our knees.
http://thetalltraveller.blogspot.com/

HOTEL ROOMS FOR TALL TRAVELERS IN THE USA
--Alan Stevens, UK. *The Tall Traveler.*

At least one hotel group has recognized the challenges faced by we tall travelers. The Hotel Monaco chain (part of Kimpton hotels) has a special range of "Tall Rooms" at sites in some large American cities.
http://bit.ly/hK2Bkq

They claim to have "longer beds, higher ceilings and doorframes, extra long bathrobes, raised showerheads, vanities and toilets". Next time I'm over there, I'll give them a try. But how is it that only one hotel chain in the world (as far as I can discover) does this? More than 15% of males, and 1% of females in Europe and the US are taller than six feet. Isn't that a market worth pursuing?
http://thetalltraveller.blogspot.com/

ALTERNATIVES TO HOTELS
Peter Greenberg videos on great places to stay.
http://bit.ly/gqjH5x,
http://bit.ly/eQ2kPe

HOTEL SECURITY
Tips from Peter Greenberg. Video.
http://bit.ly/i6O9hE

HOTELS FROM HELL
Check out TripAdvisor's "2008 Top 10 Dirtiest US and UK Hotels," chosen by their members as beyond scummy, and prepare to be utterly disgusted. See http://bit.ly/f1R5bo

VIDEO HOTEL REVIEWS
See the rooms. Unbiased hotel reviews from real travelers in video.
http://www.hotelvideoreviews.com/index.html

HOTEL BOOKING TIP
--Scott Friedman, USA.

When you book a hotel online, put a "2" in the box for Guests per Room. Ordinarily, you will be eligible for double the amenities including two breakfasts.

Then when you schedule breakfast meetings at your hotel, you will have good place to meet and your guest will think you paid extra for their meal.

"NON-SMOKING" HOTEL ROOMS
Old tobacco smoke does more than simply make a room smell stale--it can leave cancer-causing toxins behind.
http://bit.ly/cHfDCW

HIDDEN HOTEL FEES YOU CAN AVOID
In recent years, hotels have become increasingly adept at finding ways to nickel and dime their customers. According to a study published last year by PriceWaterHouseCooper's Hospitality Division, hotels are gorging themselves on surcharges and hidden fees.

Hotels worldwide were on track to rake in nearly $2-billion USD in surcharges and hidden fees in 2007, more than tripling the $550 million they took in just four years earlier. That's a lot of minibar charges and towel replacement fees.
See
http://fodors.com/news/story_2921.html

FACTOID.
Concierge. A hotel employee who attends to the needs of guests, by providing information or making arrangements, such as for theater tickets or dinner reservations.

Concierge comes from the French *comte des cierges* ("keeper of the candles"), servants who tended to traveling aristocrats in the castles of medieval France.

Fortunately, today one need not be nobility or a millionaire to get a hotel concierge to arrange the most dramatic requests.

DOES THE HOTEL CONCIERGE HAVE SECRET AGENDA?
Unbeknownst to most travelers, hotels are quietly outsourcing a core position that can make or break a guest's stay: the concierge. See
http://bit.ly/bxISFQ
http://bit.ly/bxISFQ

AIRPORT TAXIS-INTERNATIONAL
--Dan Poynter, USA.

Plan on how you will travel from the airport to your hotel.

On an around-the-world itinerary, I landed in Shanghai with two bags and an attaché case. Exiting the terminal, I searched for the taxi stand. A young woman approached me asking if I needed a cab. I dismissed her. She returned. Unable to find the taxi queue, I gave up. I thought to myself, "how dangerous could this small woman be?"

She led me to the parking structure. I asked her the price. Pretending limited English, she answered "meter." We found the car, a not-to- old Mercedes. It was clean but did not have any taxi markings. Oh well, how dangerous can she be? I put my bags in the trunk and got into the back seat.

We drove out of the parking structure. As we approached the tollbooth, she stopped, the front-passenger door opened and a man got in. I could not escape the cab since my bags were in the trunk.
My next thoughts varied between my safety and how stupid I'd been.

As we drove into Shanghai, pretending very limited English, he offered me a bottle of water. I showed I had a bottle of water. Next he offered a Handy Wipe-type towel to freshen up. I was not about to put anything on my skin or near my nose.

Again I inquired as to the price. He pointed to numbers on a card. Fortunately, I had done some research online so I knew how many RMB the fare should be. He quoted a fare four-times higher. I argued, mostly in sign language. I wrote out the amount I was willing to pay. We finally settled on a slightly higher figure. He asked for the money. I shook my head, pointed ahead and said "hotel."

As we approached the center of Shanghai, he pointed out my hotel, the Hilton. What I did not know was that the front of the hotel was being renovated and was blocked off. We had to drive down an alley and enter a side door. There were no additional hotel signs. This was not looking safe.

Again, he asked for the fare. I shook my head and motioned to the outside of the taxi.

He got out of the cab, went to the rear of the car, and waited for me. I could envision my getting out and having the female driver take off with my bags still in the trunk. So I waited until the luggage was on the steps to the hotel. Then I exited the cab, paid him, and reclaimed my bags.

Was I in any personal danger? Was there a risk of losing my luggage? Who knows? Or did my alert reactions to their every move save my day?

I felt stupid. But as we say in professional speaking, I did get a new story out of the experience.

For your first trip to an airport, go online. See the airport and your hotel's website for transportation choices. Patronize registered cabs only. In some countries, a hotel car is even safer. Ask the hotel to send a car for you. Ask them to send the name and a photograph of the driver.

HOTEL EMERGENCIES
--Norman Zalfa, International Travel Safety Expert.
nzalfa@comcast.net

When staying at a hotel, ALWAYS on the first day, walk down the emergency exit to see if the stairway is clear and you know where it leads.

Often hotels use the emergency stairway as a temporary furniture storage place and the way is blocked. Another potential problem is where the stairwell leads. Frequently it leads into a kitchen or other service area and not to the outside.

It is usually best to request a hotel room on a lower floor. Most cities do not have emergency rescue equipment capable of reaching higher floors.

Elevator rides take longer from higher floors; a consideration when the hotel has a lot of guests moving at the same time. On the other hand, if you are in a large city, the lower floors will have more street noise than upper floors. And, you will normally get better mobile phone reception on a higher floor.

SURVIVING A HOTEL FIRE
Check the fire notice on the back of the door. Then go and find the fire exits. Just looking at the map on the door is not sufficient.

If you smell smoke, ring the alarm box in the hallway or call the Front Desk immediately. Do not assume someone else will do it.
http://www.ab.ust.hk/sepo/pdf/hotelfir.PDF

Get the booklet "What to do in case of fire" at http://bit.ly/eTquhO

WHEN MAGNETIZED HOTEL KEYS LOSE THEIR MEMORY

When your key fails to unlock the door, you have to return to the Registration Desk—sometimes dragging your bags.

The memory on the keys can be damaged or cleaned off if carried close to a mobile phone, stored too close to a battery or rubbed against a magnetic device.

When checking into a hotel, request two key cards. Place the spare in your wallet. If storing the spare key in your purse, make sure it is separated from any electrical or magnetic devices.

Use the primary key card with confidence--knowing you have a backup card in reserve.

THE TRUTH ABOUT HOTEL ROOM KEYS
Is personal or sensitive information stored on them? http://bit.ly/eUPbO5, http://bit.ly/exMYoT

LOCK BUMPING
How thieves can get into your hotel room or home without a key. http://bit.ly/eorN82

See more at
http://bit.ly/cEjqes

THE ROOM WAS DARKER THAN USUAL
--Dan Poynter, a frequent flyer, USA.

Most hotel room doors do not reach to the carpeted floor. The space provides an exit for air being piped into the room. It also lets a small amount of light into the room at night, acting like a night-light.

One night I awoke with an urge to go to the bathroom. I sat up, swung my legs around, and noticed the room was unusually dark. I could not remember the direction to the bathroom and could not see the route in the dark. I rubbed my eyes and planted my feet on the floor—only to notice the carpet was unusually plush. I rubbed my eyes, tried to focus, and attempted to remember the room layout.

Then, I realized . . . surprise: I was home and in my own bedroom.

HOTEL CHALLENGES & SOLUTIONS:
The missing package.
--Dan Poynter, DanPoynter@ParaPublishing.com, USA.

What to do when the hotel "loses" the package you shipped to yourself?

You have arrived at the hotel, checked in and are told they do not have a package for you. What can you do?

Start by tracking your package online. Get the delivery date and the name of the person who signed for it. Recheck the delivery address; make sure you sent the carton to the right hotel.

Ask the front-desk person to check again.
If the response is still negative, ask him or her to call Security so you can file a report. The Security guard usually has time; he or she is not busy serving customer. And they usually have keys to every door in the building; they can get into any room where your package might be.

Tell the guard your package is missing and you would like him to look for it before you call the local police to file a theft report.
Watch him go into action!

HOTEL CHALLENGES & SOLUTIONS:
The ice machine next door.
--Dan Poynter, DanPoynter@ParaPublishing.com. USA.

You've checked into your hotel room, they gave you the last available room, it is late, you have a big day tomorrow, and you are next to the noisy ice machine. What can you do?

You could go to the business center, find a piece of paper, a felt tipped marker, and some tape.

Put the sign on the ice machine that says "Machine out of order. Please get ice on the next level."

HOTEL CHALLENGES & SOLUTIONS:
Noise next door.
--Dan Poynter, DanPoynter@ParaPublishing.com, USA.

You check into your hotel room, it is late, you are very tired, the walls are thin, and a couple in the next room is arguing at a very high volume.

You could bang on the wall, scream at them, or call Security to complain. But you know none of those remedies will work for long.

Try going next door with a smile on your face. Say to the couple: "You probably do not realize that this hotel has very thin walls. I'm embarrassed to tell you that I can hear every word that you are saying."

Not only are they likely to lower the volume, your intervention may even improve their relationship.

SPEEDING THE LIFT/ELEVATOR
—Hans Ruinemans, The Netherlands.

In a hurry? Elevator will stop at every floor?
Turn the elevator into express; go directly to your floor.

When in a hurry, enter the lift, push the Door-Close button, and push the button for your floor at the same time. Hold down both buttons for five seconds.

This works in many hotel elevators and is a trick learned from a bellman.

http://www.i-hacked.com/content/view/186/48/
http://www.youtube.com/watch?v=6dWXhxGnUi0
http://bit.ly/i5aLUq

HOTEL DRINKING GLASSES
Are hotels washing the glasses for your room? Or, are they just wiping them "clean" with a towel used by the previous guest?
Shocking video.
http://www.youtube.com/watch?v=trl6B11Jb0k

DIRTIEST ITEMS IN YOUR HOTEL ROOM
The TV remote, bedspread, telephone handset and the drinking glasses.

A video with Peter Greenburg on what actions to take.
http://www.youtube.com/watch?v=lS8VdhNETiA
http://www.youtube.com/watch?v=wlLRgt_ntbw

Peter Greenberg offers suggestions on what to do when you find yourself in a filthy hotel room.
http://www.youtube.com/watch?v=VBDi5kBoE7s

BED BUGS
Bed bugs commonly hide in mattresses, carpets, behind peeling paint or wallpaper, and in crevices in wooden furniture (like in the cracks in the wooden headboard of a bed). Bugs are nocturnal and typically bite sleeping people in an infested bed. Bugs are most active just before dawn.
http://bit.ly/fGdqD6

See the explanatory chart.
http://bit.ly/brV7yh
Finding bed bugs in a hotel. Video.
http://www.youtube.com/watch?v=4Kk7i2eiufA

The Bed Bug Registry is a free, public database of user-submitted bed bug reports from across the United States and Canada. Founded in 2006, the site has collected about 20,000 reports covering 12,000 locations.
http://bedbugregistry.com/

TIDYING UP YOUR CLOTHES
Wrinkles. Steam in the shower or blow with a hair dryer.

Lint. Need to remove hair and lint from your clothes? Forget to pack a lint roller? Take the airline tag off your checked bag, remove the backing, stick it together in a loop with the adhesive-out and roll with your hand. The super sticky adhesive will collect all the hair and lint.

Stains. Pack a few hand wipes/moist towelettes. They can be used to remove some stains from clothes. On some flights they are provided with meals. Sometimes they are in the lavatory.

✈ **FLYERTALK FORUM ON HOTELS**
Hotel Deals and building points
The place to post hotel deals conducive to "mattress running," including possible pricing errors, unusually low rates, and best price guarantees.

Note: Regularly posted deals from the chains are rarely considered good deals.
http://www.flyertalk.com/forum/hotel-deals-607/

✈ FLYERTALK FORUMS ON HOTEL REWARD PROGRAMS
http://www.flyertalk.com/forum/miles-points-1/

☺ Humor

THE PEOPLE YOU MEET IN HOTELS
Daniel Leather clothing commercial Humorous video.
http://www.youtube.com/watch?v=oDIgL4NQbNA

"**Research shows your iPhone has more bacteria on it than a toilet.**
So if you drop your iPhone into a toilet, it will come out cleaner."
--Dale Irvin, Humor Speaker.

WAKE-UP CALL
One night at an economy hotel, a professional speaker ordered a 6 AM wake-up call. The next morning, he woke before 6, but the phone did not ring until 6:30.

" Good morning," a young man said. "This is your wake-up call."

Annoyed, he let the hotel worker have it. "You were supposed to call me at 6! What if I had a $50,000 speaking opportunity this morning, and your oversight made me miss it?"

"Well, sir," the desk clerk quickly replied, "If you had a fifty-thousand dollar gig, you wouldn't be staying in this hotel, would you?"

TRAVEL DEFINITIONS

TERM	TRANSLATION
Old world charm	No bath
Tropical	Rainy
Majestic setting	A long way from town
Options galore	Nothing is included in the itinerary
Secluded hideaway	Impossible to find or get to
Pre-registered rooms	Already occupied
Explore on your own	Pay for it yourself
Knowledgeable-trip hosts	They've flown in an airplane before
No extra fees	No extras
Nominal fee	Outrageous charge
Standard	Sub-standard
Deluxe	Standard
Superior	One free shower cap
All the amenities	Two free shower caps
Plush	Top *and* bottom sheets
Gentle breezes	Occasional gale-force winds
Light and airy	No air conditioning
Picturesque	Theme park nearby
Open bar	Free ice cubes

Chapter Eighteen
On the Ground:
Cars & Trains

A. Automobile Renting/Hiring
B. Train, etc. Travel

A. Automobile Renting/Hiring

RENTING CARS IN OTHER COUNTRIES
Buying collision damage waiver insurance and liability policies when renting cars overseas can cost up to $30 USD per day but allows travelers to drive away knowing that, whatever happens, they're covered.

People who refuse rental car agency protection plans often assume they have adequate coverage through policies that insure their cars at home and generally extend to rentals. But personal auto insurance from most companies rarely applies to vehicles rented abroad. And while some credit cards offer supplemental insurance, they refuse to cover rentals in some countries.
http://nvti.ms/azNq7C

RENTING A CAR IN GERMANY—NEW RULES
Some rental agencies require an International Driver's License, available from AAA in the U.S. In

most other countries, your regular driver's license is sufficient. See
http://bit.ly/hy6fec
http://www.groupsource.com/idlp.htm

RENTAL CAR FUEL CAP LOCATIONS

Ever drive into a filling station in a rental car and wonder which side of the car the filler cap is on?

Check the fuel gauge. The filler cap is on the side with the hose on the pump pictured in the fuel gauge. e.g., it is on the driver's right-hand side of the car in the gauge pictured.

WHERE DID YOU PARK THE CAR

You are in a strange city; you can't even remember the color of the rental (hired) car. Instead of jotting your parking location on a scrap of paper, which can get misplaced, take a picture of the parking location sign with your camera phone or PDA.

Or get an iPhone App such as G-Park.

iPHONE APPS

SpeedAlert.
With this App, your iPhone will alert you when your car exceeds a pre-set speed. You select the warning sound. Free. Visit the App Store.

Speedometer uses GPS to register your current speed, average speed, and top speed in both mph and kph.
See the App Store.

CITIES WITH THE WORST TRAFFIC; PLACES TO AVOID
Congestion consumes billions of gallons of fuel, wastes hundreds of billions of dollars in productivity, and causes billions of stress headaches. Yet more than 100 million automobile commuters each day feel they have few options.

There are four reasons for America's congestion problem, also applicable to most European and Asian economies: first, most of us work during the same hours of the day; second, the country's economic success has allowed households to buy multiple cars; third, there are more people now than when most roadways were conceived; fourth, more cars means more accidents which means more delays.
http://bit.ly/d5zJmh

CARS COST MORE AT AIRPORTS
The rental rates are significantly higher at airports, and rental companies often tack on fees such as an "airport concession" or a similar charge. See explanation and comparison chart.
http://bit.ly/aaBnDa

CAR RENTAL/CAR HIRE TIP
Protect yourself by taking photos of your rental car with your mobile phone. Photograph close-ups of any damage before out drive out of the lot. Take photos

again when you return the car. That will allow you to dispute any claim by the rental company that you damaged its vehicle.

CAR RENTAL TIPS
Video with Peter Greenberg.
http://www.youtube.com/watch?v=Qi24u82E_ww

CAR RENTAL PROGRAMS/PARTNERS
http://www.flyertalk.com/forum/miles-points-1/

AIRPORT SHUTTLES
The GO Group provides airport shuttles at more than 50 airports in the United States, Canada, Mexico, Scotland, England, France, and Italy.
http://goairportshuttle.com/

B. Train, etc. Travel

CLASSES OF TRAINS IN EUROPE
There are generally two seating classes, known as "First Class" and "Second Class", or the equivalent in the local language. In Britain Second Class is known as "Standard Class". Third class was abolished in most European countries in the 1950s.

A system used by most European railway companies is that the First Class section of a train is marked in yellow, usually a yellow band above the doors &/or the windows.

SAVING ON TRAVEL
A Peter Greenberg video.
http://www.youtube.com/watch?v=SKc5WcboBy4

LEGENDARY TRAINS
A Peter greenberg video.
http://www.youtube.com/watch?v=-CeGLw8h_C4

VIDEOS OF CRUISE SHIP ACTIVITIES
http://bit.ly/gJvDLv

☺Humor

JERRY SEINFELD ON CAR RESERVATIONS
Video.
http://www.youtube.com/watch?v=A7uvttu8ct0

A THIEF IN PARIS
--Ira Rimson, USA.

A thief in Paris planned to steal some paintings from the Louvre. After careful planning, he got past security, stole the paintings, and made it safely to his van.

However, he was captured only two blocks away when his van ran out of gas.

When asked how he could mastermind such a crime and then make such an obvious error, he replied, "Monsieur that is the reason I stole the paintings. I need Monet to buy Degas to make the Van Gogh."

And you thought we didn't have De Gaulle to reprint this story.

Well, I figured we have nothing Toulouse.

THE TRAIN HAS FAILED

A large two-engine train was crossing the U.S. After they had gone some distance, one of the engines broke down. "No problem," the engineer thought, and carried on at half power.

Farther on down the line, the other engine broke down, and the train came to a standstill.

The engineer decided he should inform the passengers about why the train had stopped, and made the following announcement:

"Ladies and gentlemen, I have some good news and some bad news. The bad news is that both engines have failed, and we will be stuck here for some time.

The good news is that you decided to take the train and are not on a plane."

Chapter Nineteen
Expressing Yourself
Writing and Speaking About Your Travel

You can help other people, celebrate your travel, get great treatment, and make money from what you learn traveling. Travel provides opportunities to learn and to share. Two ways to share your knowledge, research, and experiences are writing and professional speaking.

A. Writing about your travel
B. Speaking about your travel

A. Writing about your travel

Travel writing is a genre that may cover real or imaginary places. Categories may range from the documentary to the evocative, from literary to journalistic, and from the humorous to the serious.

When we think of travel writing, we usually think of tourism, guidebooks, and reviews.

Travel writing that is valued as literature in its own right may be referred to as travel literature.
http://en.wikipedia.org/wiki/Travel_writing

"When your parents taught you not to write in books, they did not know they were raising an author who would autograph them."

A World Tourism Organization study predicts an expansion in world travel; by 2020 it is expected that travel will be the world's largest industry.

This is great news for travel writers and publishers who can direct their publications to different kinds of travelers: business, adventurers, families on vacation, etc., as well as to various areas of interest, such as U.S., Europe or Canada. There is even "special interest travel"—a term that can mean anything from eco-tourism to adventure travel to motoring through Canada by RV.

Travel publishers are taking large general-coverage books and cutting them into several special-focus books.

Many people today are taking more frequent but shorter vacations. This accounts for the growth of books on weekend getaways or short hikes.

Few people are full-time travel writers. Most supplement their income and their lust for journeying to far-away places with what becomes paid travel.

Here are some tips for writing about travel: Be patient and persistent. If you find other writers going after the same story, adjust. Find a unique angle. Be prepared. Learn the history and become an expert on the area. Inject humor to make the story light and enjoyable.

Travel publications are always looking for humor. Try to stand out from the crowd. Your story needs a personal voice and a point of view. Say something new about your subject. What is it about the place that impressed or depressed you? Avoid trite phrases and think of creative descriptions. Use a thesaurus to find alternative words.

CITIZEN JOURNALISM
What are people reading now?
A Peter Greenberg video.
http://www.youtube.com/watch?v=86L0_j0m-AE

1. Books

There are books on how to write, produce, and promote travel books and articles. See *Books In Print* and Amazon.com for a listing. Get all that apply to your type of travel book. Buy used copies from Amazon. Often they sell for pennies plus shipping. You need the books for research, not for display.

It is far cheaper to buy these books than to make one mistake. Learn from the experience of others; do not reinvent the wheel.

See the *Travel Writer's Guide* by Gordon Burgett.
http://www.gordonburgett.com/

2. Reports

For more details on travel writing, publishing and promoting, see Document 616, Travel Books at http://ParaPublishing.com

3. Travel Writers Associations

The Society of American Travel Writers
http://www.satw.org

North American Travel Journalists Association (NATJA)
http://natja.org

Travel Writers Association
Http://www.TravelWritersAssociation.org

Australian Society of Travel Writers
http://astw.org.au

British Guild of Travel Writers
http://www.bgtw.org

Travel Media Association of Canada
http://www.travelmedia.ca/

BC Association of Travel Writers
http://www.bctravelwriters.com/

Independent Book Publishers Association
http://www.IBPA-Online.org

4. Other contacts
http://www.travelwriters.com/

INFOKITS
Detailed information on book writing, production and promotion.
http://parapublishing.com/sites/para/resources/infokit.cfm

***PUBLISHING POYNTERS* NEWSLETTER**
Free *Publishing Poynters* ezine. Full of tips and resources on book writing, publishing and promoting. Subscribe and get past issues.
http://parapublishing.com/sites/para/resources/newsletter.cfm

DAN POYNTER SPEAKS ON BOOK WRITING, PUBLISHING AND PROMOTING
Speech Descriptions
http://parapublishing.com/sites/para/speaking/speechdesc.cfm

COMPLETE LIST OF FREE AND FOR-SALE DOCUMENTS
Book Writing, Publishing and Promoting
http://DanSentMe.com/sites/para/resources/allproducts.cfm

B. Speaking about your travel

1. Resources for Speakers
2. Speaking Tips
3. Organizations/Associations for Speakers
4. Meetings Industry

FACTOID
More than 14 percent of the world's population speaks Mandarin Chinese as a first language; 5 percent of the world's population speaks English as a first language. More people in the world speak English as a second language than any other.

1. Resources for Speakers
Fees, bureaus, meeting planners, coaching, statistics, etc

For even more information, there are professional speaking associations and chapters in more than ten countries.

SPEECH DEFINITIONS
--Dan Poynter, USA.

When is a "keynote" not a keynote? Conventions and other events usually consist of general sessions, breakout sessions, and a single keynote address. A general-session address on the second day of the event is not a "keynote." Here are definitions and explanations.

Keynote address: The initial general-session speech from the main platform that welcomes attendees, introduces the theme, and sets the tone for the event.

The speaker may go on to talk about the industry, tell his or her story, etc. It should be the most important speech at a convention or meeting. See http://bit.ly/b2dm0m

General Session: A main-platform speech on any (hopefully relevant) subject shared with all event attendees. There are no other speeches being delivered to compete with it. An example is a speech delivered after a meal.

Split-General Session: when two main speeches are being delivered simultaneously. In some cases, the main auditorium is split down the middle by drawing an air wall. Attendees select one presentation or the other.

Breakout Session: A concurrent speech or workshop delivered at the same time as other presentations.

Most conventions have one keynote, several general sessions and many breakout sessions.

DEFINITIONS: Agents and Bureaus.
--Stef Du Plessis, South Africa.

In some countries, the terms *agent* and *bureau* are used interchangeably. In other countries, a distinction is made between the two.

Agents work for speakers. They represent individual speakers.

Bureaus work for meeting planners. They find speakers for events.

GROSS FEES vs NET FEES
What does your speaking-bureau contract say?
-Kristin Arnold, NSA/US President 2010-2011.

Bureaus and agents may pay you on the gross or the net. The difference can be a lot of money. The International Association of Speakers Bureaus (IASB) defines the terms as follows:

Gross Fee
The total fee the buyer is charged for a booking, including agents' fees, but excluding speaker expenses (air and ground transportation, tips, hotels, and meals.) Bureau commissions are not paid on expenses

Net Fee
The amount of the fee the speaker will actually receive for a booking after agency or bureau fees and before expenses.

So here's Kristin's understanding of the terms:

A "gross fee" speaker has a fee that the bureau and speaker agree to. The bureau or event organizer can charge whatever they want to on top of that. The bureau then remits the entire gross fee to the speaker.

A "net fee" speaker has a fee that the bureau and speaker agree to. The bureau or event organizer takes a percentage (often 30%) of that fee (NOT including expenses) and remits the remainder to the speaker.

Either model is completely acceptable--but it's all about transparency between the speaker and the bureau, so that there are no surprises or misunderstandings.

SPEAKING INDUSTRY LINGO/JARGON
The professional speaking industry has its own terminology.
http://bit.ly/gNj9LP

POLITICIANS AND HIGH SPEAKING FEES
--Noel Griese, *The Southern Review of Books* newsletter published monthly by Anvil Publishers. USA.

Talk may be cheap, but not if you're a past president of the United States.

Bill Clinton reported earning $6 million for speaking engagements in 2008, and has been paid as much as $350,000 for a single appearance, although most of his appearances netted him only $125,000 each.

Bill Clinton's post-presidential income was derived almost entirely from foreign companies, according to filings made by his wife after her nomination to be

When George W. Bush arrived in Calgary for his maiden speech as the former U.S. leader, he racked up at least $100,000 in fees.
Bush was booked for 10 more speeches after Calgary, to be delivered in the U.S. and other countries.

Richard Nixon, the most disgraced U.S. president in recent history, earned $600,000 from broadcaster David Frost for 24 hours of taped interviews in 1977. A decade later, Nixon charged a single interview fee of $6,000, or so his handlers told the *Toronto Star* when a request was made for an hour of his time.

Ronald Reagan, a revered leader, capitalized on his reputation as the Great Communicator from the podium, raking in $2 million from a Japanese industrial firm for two 20-minute speeches he made in Japan in 1989.

In 1979, former President Gerald Ford was paid $12,000, plus expenses (a private jet), to speak at a Richland Chamber of Commerce luncheon in the Eastern Washington city.

Past-President George H.W. Bush, father of the 43rd president, made millions on the lecture circuit and served as a rainmaker for U.S. investors in the Middle East.

Secretary of State Clinton's highest fee of $350,000 was received from a Kuwaiti bank. Canada has been a particular cash cow for Clinton.

George W. Bush is represented by the Washington Speakers Bureau. The past president's wife, former first lady Laura Bush, can also be booked through the Washington Speakers Bureau.

Former New York Mayor Rudy Giuliani cashed in on his celebrity by giving many speeches after 9/11.

According to the *New York Daily News*, Giuliani took in more than $11 million over a two-year period.
http://bit.ly/aERgmj
http://bit.ly/axbtFy
http://bit.ly/acXTby

Editor's comment: When a politician receives a high book advance or a high speaking fee, one has to wonder if an organization is buying influence while getting around campaign-finance laws by labeling donations as book or speech fees.

INTERNATIONAL ASSOCIATION OF SPEAKERS BUREAUS
See the directory of the International Association of Speakers Bureaus (IASB).

IASB (formerly the International Group of Agencies and Bureaus) is the worldwide trade association of speaker agencies and bureaus, with bureau members in Australia, Canada, Colombia, England, Germany, Ireland, Mexico, The Netherlands, South Korea, Spain, Singapore, Brasil, France, Portugal and New Zealand as well as the United States. Founded in 1986, IASB is to the speaking-bureau industry what MPI is to meeting professionals. IASB member bureaus subscribe to a Code of Ethics, take part in on-going professional development, and adhere to a high level of professional standards.
http://www.iasbweb.org/

REACH 27 BUREAUS IN AUSTRALIA AND NEW ZEALAND
Free or paid listing. See
http://www.bioview.com.au/
http://www.bioviewUSA.com

MEETING PLANNER RESOURCES
http://bit.ly/9PX4Vj

SPEAKERNET NEWS
A free weekly newsletter full of tips and resources on professional speaking. Highly recommended.
To subscribe, see http://www.speakernetnews.com

THE MEDIA COACH NEWSLETTER
Delivered directly to your inbox every Friday morning, "The MediaCoach" by Alan Stevens is packed with hints, tips, and advice on every aspect of communication skills. See
http://www.mediacoach.co.uk/free_email_newsletter.htm

RESOURCES FOR SPEAKERS.
--Frank Furness, UK.
See http://www.frankfurnessresources.com/

STATISTICS TO QUOTE
World statistics—updated in real time. Watch the numbers grow. http://www.worldometers.info/

RESOURCES AND LINKS FOR THE INTERNATIONAL SPEAKER
Tips you will want to print out; websites you will want to bookmark. http://www.globalspeakers.net/

NUMBERS ON PROFESSIONAL SPEAKING
Statistics on the professional speaking and meeting industries.
http://www.SpeakingStatistics.com
http://bit.ly/cmWjP1
http://bit.ly/bEzZ3n

2. Speaking Tips

DOES YOUR AUDIENCE UNDERSTAND YOU?
--Dan Poynter, USA.

If you normally speak with a regional dialect of English or thick accent and are speaking outside of your own region, pay special attention to your pronunciation.

We are professional speakers and professionals want to make sure each member of the audience understands the message. Also make sure that more than just more than just your home audience will appreciate your humor.

Regional accents can be fun for a sentence or two. After that the audience finds them tedious and even incomprehensible.

If you aren't communicating your message, you aren't earning your money as a speaker.

BE UNDERSTOOD--DISCOVER GLOBAL ENGLISH
Globish ("Global English") is M. Nerriere's answer to the challenges of idiomatic English. Nerriere noticed

that non-Anglophones would communicate happily among themselves until the British or American speaker began what was often a soporific monologue.

These foreign speakers were terrified to ask for clarification and generally were lulled into boredom, especially if the accent was difficult and the diction too fast.

Figures of speech feature prominently in the repertoires of Anglophones and if you present to an audience of native speakers, have fun with them! But ask first if there are any non-Anglophones present and modify accordingly. Also remember that British idiom differs from American and Australia figures of speech.

See Elizabeth Noble's article:
http://www.ennobler.net/Globish.html

SPEAKERS CONNECT WITH GLOBISH
--Elizabeth Noble, Panama.
If you use English that is too dense or too subtle, if you have ever said, "fly in the ointment," "bird in the hand" or used "Band-Aid" as a metaphor, you could be losing your audience—and business.

See *Winners Speak Globish*. In it, Elizabeth Noble explains the challenges speakers face with international audiences and provides solutions.

You will Discover how to
- Be understood everywhere
- Show respect for diversity
- Include your entire audience
- Encourage group interaction
- Promote feedback to you
- Increase client satisfaction
- Win profitable new business
- Get invited back

Just $7.75, USD for the download in a variety of eBook formats. For details and ordering, see http://www.smashwords.com/books/view/19008

CHALLENGES & SOLUTIONS:
Screaming kid in your audience.
--Dan Poynter, http://ParaPublishing.com, USA.

The noise is interrupting your message and disturbing your audience. You know if you make an issue with the mother, the audience could side with her. What would you do?

One speaker approached the mother and said "Excuse me, I just rec'd a signal from the AV people. They are recording this session and the background noise is interfering with their work. Please take your baby out of the room until it quiets down."

(Sometimes it helps to shift the blame.)

CHALLENGES & SOLUTIONS:
She took the call.
--Dan Seidman, http://www.salesautopsy.com/, USA.

I was recently giving a keynote speech to 350 financial services pros when a woman in the front of the audience answered her phone and, not wanting to disturb her tablemates, walked up to the front of the platform, and began her dialogue behind me, but in front of the video screen! Huh?

I walked up along side her and held my microphone next to her. The conversation boomed through the audience. The combination broadcast of their laughter and her voice woke this woman up and she slithered away, a more conscientious cell phone user.

CHALLENGES & SOLUTIONS:
Disruptive young audience.

The teenage audience was multitasking: texting, talking and (presumably) listening. The speaker was annoyed, offended, and frustrated.

He stopped and announced: "I don't care if you choose to quiet down or leave the room but it is not considerate or fair for you to disrupt the experience for your neighbors."

THE TOP TEN BEST PRESENTATIONS—EVER.
http://bit.ly/dgsuck

MEN, BUTTON YOUR JACKET
--Sandy Dumont, The Image Architect, USA.

Jackets are designed to be buttoned. You will look better if you close up your coat while presenting.

If like many male presenters you have a bit of a tummy, the buttoned jacket will hide it.

As a speaker, you are in front of the room and everyone is looking at you for the entire speech. You want to look your best. An audience member that doesn't like the way you dress stops listening to your message. Button up.

INTERPRETER NOT TRANSLATOR
--Alan Parisse, Canada.

Translators work with the written word; interpreters with the spoken word. Many speech interpreters do not like being referred to as a "translator".

SPEAKERS SPEAK OUT
Videos of speakers being interviewed about speaking. http://bit.ly/hqMTS8

TOP TEN LISTS
These suggestions apply to speaking too. See http://topten.org/

THE EXPAT LIFE
A Wall Street Journal Forum on working away from home.
http://bit.ly/9YwdjQ

CHAMBER OF COMMERCE
--Scott Friedman, Scott@FunnyScott.com, USA.

A great place for U.S. speakers to start on speaking globally: AmCham (American Chamber of Commerce). After speaking for free at one of their monthly meetings in Bangkok, I made many contacts that led to future seminars in Thailand.
www.uschamber.com/international/directory

3. Organizations/Associations for Speakers

ORGANIZATION

Global Speakers Federation (GSF) is a **federation** of speaking associations from around the world.
http://www.globalspeakers.net/

Visit these sites for the latest information on professional speaking internationally.

Asian Professional Speakers/Singapore (APS/S)
http://www.asiaspeakers.org/apss/

Canadian Association of Professional Speakers (CAPS)
http://canadianspeakers.org/

German Speakers Association (GSA)
http://www.germanspeakers-association.de/

Malaysian Professional Speakers (MAPS)
http://www.maps.org.my/

National Speakers Association/US (NSA/US)
http://www.NSAspeaker.org

National Speakers Association/Australia (NSAA)
http://www.nationalspeakers.asn.au/

PSA/Holland (PSA/H)
http://www.psaholland.org/

Professional Speakers Association of the UK and Ireland. PSA/UK.
http://www.professionalspeakersassociation.co.uk/

NSA/New Zealand (NSA/NZ
http://www.nationalspeakers.org.nz/

PSA/Southern Africa (PSASA)
http://www.psasouthernafrica.co.za

l'Association Française des Conférenciers Professionnels (AFCP).
http://www.association-conferenciers.com/

Global Speakers Network (GSN) is an exclusive **network**ing group of professionals who speak internationally.

Join GSN (for those speaking internationally)
http://www.globalspeakers.net/network

GSF Website/Online Resources
http://www.globalspeakers.net/

GSF *NewsBrief.* (GSN members only).
Dan Poynter, USA, editor.
http://www.globalspeakers.net/share/channel/newsbrief

GSN LinkedIn Community Group (For those speaking internationally and those wishing to speak in other countries.)
Erwin Van Lun, Moderator.
http://www.linkedin.com/e/gis/1080047

The GSF/Global Speakers Network helps meeting planners to find speakers.
Check your listing at
http://bureau.espeakers.com/ifps/

Where in the World (find other GSN members when you travel)
http://www.espeakers.com/witw/

FINDING SPEAKING OPPORTUNITIES IN OTHER COUNTRIES.
--Ed Rigsbee, USA and Lindsay Adams, Australia.

One way to line up international speaking engagements is to contact other speakers on your subject.

When contacting speakers for help in getting gigs in their country, start by offering your help in getting gigs for them in your own country.

Log onto the following websites and search for speakers on your subject (search by category). They know the meeting planners in their geographic area that are buying your topic. Offer to introduce them to the right people in your country. Remember, we are conspirators not competitors.

SPEAKING EAGLES: professional speakers who fly. The Speaking Eagles is an affinity group within NSA/US. While most of the members are pilots, membership is open to anyone with an affiliation to aviation. There are skydivers, balloonists, flight attendants, fixed-base operators, and professionals who speak to aviation groups. A number of NSA members fly for business, sport and pleasure.

Speaking Eagles founder Howard Putnam is a former CEO of Southwest Airlines.

The Eagles meet during the National Speakers Association convention and winter events.
To join/attend or FMI, contact Howard Putnam, HowardDP@aol.com

4. Meetings Industry

HOW MEETING PLANNERS SELECT INTERNATIONAL VENUES
One would think a lot of planning goes into selecting a foreign meeting site but that is rarely the case. Most selection is random. http://bit.ly/9fvnns

CONVENTION BAG TAG

Mark your convention bag so that it will not look like the rest. Avoid having it picked up by mistake. Carefully peal the airline tag off your (checked) luggage handle and apply it to the handle of the bag. In addition to routing and bar codes, the tag displays your name.

The adhesive on the tag can also substitute for a lint pickup when required. Slowly and carefully separate the ends and blot with the adhesive.

MEETING PLANNER RESOURCES
http://bit.ly/9PX4Vj

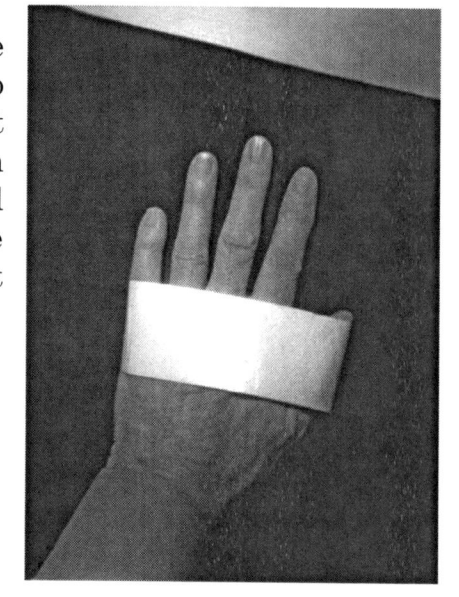

MEETING INDUSTRY NEWS.
MICEpoint is the leading marketplace for the worldwide meetings industry. Buyers and organizers can browse and search the large and detailed listing of MICE industry suppliers for f.r.e.e. See http://bit.ly/gQ09hd

☺ Humor

THE STATE OF THE MEETINGS INDUSTRY.
--Joe Malarky & Joe Calloway, USA.

The meetings industry has been under the weather for a little while, but it's coming back to life!
http://www.youtube.com/watch?v=B7ADUZBKUq8

Colophon

This book was completely produced using the New Model production system described in *Writing Nonfiction: Turning Thoughts Into Books* by Dan Poynter. See the book at Amazon.com.

Writing and manuscript building
Manuscript preparation
MS-Word on a MacBook Air.

Cover design
Robert Howard Graphic Design

Typefaces:
Body text: Century, 12 pt.
Chapter titles/subtitles: Century 18 pt. Bold.

Conversion to eBook
Preparation by Elizabeth Beeton
Conversion to eBook editions by Smashwords.com

Publishing
Para Publishing, Santa Barbara, USA.

Distribution
eBook:
Smashwords.com
Amazon.com, B&N.com and other eBook resellers.
Printed book:
National Book Network

Dan Poynter Speaks on Air Travel

He is available to educate and entertain your group.

Convention attendees travel (they had to get there.)

Speech Descriptions
http://bit.ly/aZhiqm

DanPoynter@ParaPublishing.com

http://airtravelhandbook.com/

QUICK ORDER FORM

Satisfaction guaranteed

To get another copy of this book, see below.
Inquire about discounts for multiple orders.

Online orders:
Printed book: Amazon.com

eBook:
http://www.smashwords.com/books/view/24746
It is also a Kindle book at Amazon.

Telephone orders:
Call +1(800) PARAPUB toll free
(+1-800-727-2782).
Have your credit card ready.

For more information on our other books, seminars, speaking and consulting, see
http://ParaPublishing.com
http://AirTravelHandbook.com

To be notified of updates for this book, send your name, Zip Code or country, and your email address to Becky@ParaPublishing.com

You can be mentioned in the next edition of this book.
Send in your tips and/or corrections to
Info@ParaPublishing.com

WITHDRAWN

JUN 2012